Implementation in a Longitudinal Sample of New American Schools

Four Years into Scale-Up

Sheila Nataraj Kirby
Mark Berends
Scott Naftel

Supported by
New American Schools

RAND
EDUCATION

The research described in this report was supported by New American Schools.

Library of Congress Cataloging-in-Publication Data

Kirby, Sheila Nataraj, 1946-
    Implementation in a longitudinal sample of New American Schools : four years
into scale-up / Sheila Nataraj Kirby, Mark Berends, Scott Naftel.
        p. cm.
    "MR-1413."
    Includes bibliographical references.
    ISBN 0-8330-3060-4
    1. New American Schools (Organization) 2. School improvement programs—
United States—Evaluation. 3. Educational change—United States. I. Berends,
Mark, 1962– II. Naftel, Scott, 1952– III. Title.

LB2822.82 .K524 2001
370'.973—dc21

                                                              2001048312

RAND is a nonprofit institution that helps improve policy and decisionmaking through research and analysis. RAND® is a registered trademark. RAND's publications do not necessarily reflect the opinions or policies of its research sponsors.

Published 2001 by RAND
1700 Main Street, P.O. Box 2138, Santa Monica, CA 90407-2138
1200 South Hayes Street, Arlington, VA 22202-5050
201 North Craig Street, Suite 102, Pittsburgh, PA 15213
RAND URL: http://www.rand.org/
To order RAND documents or to obtain additional information,
contact Distribution Services: Telephone: (310) 451-7002;
Fax: (310) 451-6915; Email: order@rand.org

As a private nonprofit corporation, New American Schools (NAS) began in 1991 to fund the development of designs aimed at transforming entire schools at the elementary and secondary levels. After competition and development phases, NAS currently is scaling up its designs to form a critical mass of schools within partnering districts. During this phase, RAND's research activities include monitoring the progress of a sample of NAS schools in seven partnering jurisdictions through the 1999–2000 school year.

This is one in a series of reports aimed at those who want to better understand the burgeoning area of whole-school or comprehensive school reform, and is one of two reports focusing on trends in implementation in a longitudinal sample of NAS schools. This report is the follow-on report to M. Berends, S. N. Kirby, S. Naftel, and C. McKelvey, *Implementation and performance in New American Schools: Three years into scale-up* (2001). This earlier report also provided a look at performance in these NAS schools.

Other RAND reports and articles about NAS include:

New American Schools' concept of break the mold designs: How designs evolved over time and why, by Susan Bodilly, 2001 (MR-1288-NAS).

Implementation and performance in New American Schools: Three years into scale-up, by Mark Berends, Sheila Nataraj Kirby, Scott Naftel, and Christopher McKelvey, 2001 (MR-1145-EDU).

"Teacher-reported effects of New American Schools' designs: Exploring relationships to teacher background and school contex," by Mark Berends, *Educational evaluation and policy analysis*, 2000, 22(1), pp. 65–82.

"Necessary district support for comprehensive school reform" by Susan J. Bodilly and Mark Berends. In Gary Orfield and Elizabeth H. DeBray (eds.), *Hard work for good schools: Facts not fads in Title I reform*. Boston: Civil Rights Project, Harvard University, 1999, pp. 111–119.

Assessing the progress of New American Schools: A status report, by Mark Berends, 1999 (MR-1085-ED).

Lessons from New American Schools' scale-up phase: Prospects for bringing designs to multiple schools, by Susan J. Bodilly, 1998 (MR-942-NAS).

New American Schools after six years, by Thomas K. Glennan, Jr., 1998 (MR-945-NAS).

Funding comprehensive school reform, by Brent R. Keltner, 1998 (IP-175-EDU).

Reforming America's schools: Observations on implementing "whole school designs," by Susan J. Bodilly and Thomas K. Glennan, 1998 (RB-8016-EDU).

Lessons from New American Schools Development Corporation's demonstration phase, by Susan J. Bodilly, 1996 (MR-729-NASDC).

Reforming and conforming: NASDC principals discuss school accountability systems, by Karen Mitchell, 1996 (MR-716-NASDC).

"Lessons learned from RAND's Formative Assessment of NASDC's Phase 2 Demonstration effort," by Susan J. Bodilly. In Sam Stringfield, Steven Ross, and Lana Smith (eds.), *Bold Plans for School Restructuring: The New American Schools Designs*. Mahwah, NJ: Lawrence Erlbaum Associates, 1996, pp. 289–324.

Designing New American Schools: Baseline observations on nine design teams, by Susan J. Bodilly, Susanna Purnell, Kimberly Ramsey, and Christina Smith, 1995 (MR-598-NASDC).

Funding for this research was provided under a contract with NAS and was supported by the Ford Foundation and another donor. This report was written under the aegis of RAND Education.

CONTENTS

FIGURES

TABLES

SUMMARY

As a response to the school reforms that had produced little change in the nation's test scores, New American Schools (NAS) launched its efforts for whole-school reform in 1991. As a private nonprofit organization, NAS's mission is to help schools and districts significantly raise the achievement of large numbers of students with whole-school designs and the assistance design teams provide during the implementation process. NAS is currently in the scale-up phase of its effort in which the designs are being widely diffused in partnering jurisdictions across the nation.

An earlier report, Berends, Kirby, et al. (2001), provided an overview of the progress in implementation and performance in a longitudinal sample of schools three years into the scale-up phase. This current report provides an update on the progress in implementation one year later in a longitudinal sample of schools adopting one of seven designs:

- Audrey Cohen College [AC] (currently renamed Purpose-Centered Education);

- Authentic Teaching, Learning, and Assessment for All Students [AT];

- Co-NECT Schools [CON];

- Expeditionary Learning Outward Bound [EL];

- Modern Red Schoolhouse [MRSH];

- National Alliance for Restructuring Education [NARE] (currently renamed America's Choice Design Network); and

- Roots & Wings [RW].

The report is based on a variety of data gathered from the schools: principal and teacher surveys conducted during the 1996–1997, 1997–1998, and 1998–1999 school years, and data provided by districts on school demographic characteristics. In addition, the report relies on other RAND studies that included site visits to schools and school districts to gather information about district and school administrators' and teachers' reports of the progress of the NAS initiative (Bodilly, 1998).

LIMITATIONS OF THE STUDY

There are some important limitations of this research that need to be kept in mind. The sample of schools analyzed here consisted of, for most design teams, the first schools to which they had provided assistance with implementing their designs on a fee-for-service basis. There were many changes in both the designs and the assistance provided as the teams and the schools gained experience (see Bodilly, 2001). Thus, when interpreting the findings in this report, it is important to note the unique features of the population of schools we have studied.

THE ANALYSIS SAMPLE

The target population of schools for this study was all schools beginning implementation of a NAS design during school year 1995–1996 or 1996–1997 in seven jurisdictions that chose to partner with NAS at the beginning of the scale-up phase: Cincinnati, Dade, Kentucky, Memphis, Philadelphia, San Antonio, and Washington state.

The schools in the sample were located in largely urban, high-poverty and high-minority districts.

The analysis sample for the earlier study consisted of 104 schools that were implementing in both 1997 and 1998 and which had com-

plete data from both principals and teachers in both years. These schools were followed up a year later; only 71 of the 104 schools responded. A few of the schools had dropped the design but the majority of the attrition in the sample was due to nonresponse. This is not unusual in panel data. Thus, the analysis sample for the current study consists of 71 schools in which principals reported that they were implementing designs in all three years (1997, 1998, and 1999) and which had complete data (i.e., from teachers and principals) in all three years. Despite the smaller sample size, our findings are remarkably robust and mirror those found in our earlier study (Berends, Kirby, et al., 2001). The teacher sample consisted of approximately 1,500 teachers.

TRENDS IN IMPLEMENTATION

As measured by teacher reports on our indicators in our longitudinal sample of NAS schools, implementation increased and deepened over the first four years after schools adopted designs, although at a decreasing rate. Between the fourth and fifth years, however, we found a significant downturn in implementation, although a few schools with more years of implementation continued to show progress in implementation.

Implementation increased modestly from 1997 to 1999 across all schools by about 3/10ths of a standard deviation. The between-school variance declined slightly over this time period, as measured by the standard deviation, although the within-school variance increased slightly.

FACTORS AFFECTING IMPLEMENTATION

We decomposed the variance in implementation into its variance components: within-school variance and between-school variance. The variance in implementation within schools was much larger than the variance between schools. In fact, only 18 percent of the total variance in reported teacher implementation was between schools; the remaining 82 percent was within schools. The between-school variance component declined from 27 percent in 1998 to 18 percent in 1999, with a corresponding increase in the within-school variance component.

Our multilevel models explained almost all of the between-school variance and about 31 percent of the within-school variance.

The findings are largely consistent with those of our earlier study (Berends, Kirby, et al., 2000).

Principal Leadership

Principal leadership was the single most important predictor in the models, both at the teacher level and the school level.[1] Schools in which teachers reported strong principal leadership also reported much higher levels of implementation, by over half a standard deviation. Teachers who rated their principals higher than others in the same school also reported significantly higher levels of implementation (again by over half a standard deviation). We find that this variable was strongly correlated with teacher reports of the level of resources—in terms of materials, funds, and time—available to them to implement designs.

Prior Levels of Implementation

We find that schools with higher levels of prior implementation in 1997 tended to make steady progress over time. This finding, while not surprising, highlights the importance of making sure that schools are off to a good start. Without this, schools are likely to fall further behind as time passes.

Teacher Perceptions

Not surprisingly, teacher perceptions of students and their readiness to learn were all significantly related to level of implementation. Teachers reporting that lack of basic skills was not a hindrance to

---

[1]Teachers were asked several questions regarding the degree of support and leadership provided by the principal. These included communicating clearly what is expected of teachers, demonstrating supportive and encouraging behavior, getting resources for the school, enforcing rules for student conduct, talking with teachers regarding instructional practices, having confidence in the expertise of the teachers, and taking a personal interest in the professional development of teachers. We combined these into a summative index of principal leadership.

their students' academic success, that lack of student discipline and parent support was not a problem, or that students can learn with the resources available also reported higher implementation than those who felt otherwise. African American teachers also reported higher levels of implementation than non–African American teachers.

School Characteristics

Implementation was higher in high-poverty schools as well as schools serving high numbers of minority students. However, in schools that served significant numbers of *both* poor and minority students, implementation levels were significantly lower.

Designs and Design Team Assistance

Our results emphasize the importance of design-related factors and design team assistance. High reported levels of implementation were related to reportedly clear communication by design teams and higher levels of teacher support for the designs. In addition, we do find that the types of designs themselves were important, with some such as CON, NARE, and RW clearly reporting higher implementation, and others such as MRSH reporting significantly lower levels of implementation. Controlling for other factors including prior implementation levels, AC schools showed marked progress over this time period.

District Support

There were large differences in implementation between jurisdictions. In general, implementation was higher in those districts that were more supportive of the NAS designs and characterized by stability of district leadership (e.g., Memphis). Controlling for other factors, including prior implementation levels, we found that there were no significant differences among jurisdictions by 1999, with two exceptions. San Antonio schools were about 6/10ths of a standard deviation and Washington schools about half a standard deviation lower on the implementation index relative to Memphis schools.

Both of these jurisdictions ranked low with respect to district support.

Based on all of RAND's work, it is fair to infer that district and institutional factors are extremely important in ensuring the success of comprehensive school reform, particularly in the early stages of implementing the designs.

Funding

Our exit interviews with 30 principals of schools that had dropped the NAS designs as well as other related RAND research highlight the importance of adequate resources in funding. Lack of funding was the single most important reason cited by close to three-quarters of the schools in the decision to drop the design.

CONCLUSIONS AND POLICY IMPLICATIONS

NAS and the design teams partnered with schools and districts that are characterized by a host of problems related to poverty, achievement, and climate characteristics. To scale-up the designs or replicate implementation in these sites is extremely difficult. Implementation varied both within and across schools, sites, and designs.

It is clear that several factors need to be aligned for designs to be well-implemented in schools. Without strong principal leadership, without teachers who support the designs and have a strong sense of teacher efficacy, without district leadership and support, without clear communication and provision of materials and staff support on the part of design teams, implementation is likely to lag far behind. These are sobering and important lessons for federal, state, and local efforts aimed at comprehensive school reform.

Our findings also suggest that comprehensive school reform faces many obstacles during implementation, and because of this, whole-school designs face continuing challenges in ultimately achieving their main purpose: significantly raising the achievement of all students.

ACKNOWLEDGMENTS

A research project such as this is never accomplished without the collaboration and cooperation of many people and organizations. We would like to thank the Ford Foundation and another donor for providing the research funding to NAS to support RAND's ongoing assessment. We are grateful to our reviewers, Robert Croninger, University of Maryland, and Amanda Datnow, University of Toronto. The report benefited greatly, both in substance and clarity, from their comments.

NAS, as an advocate for school reform, deserves a special acknowledgement for supporting independent research on its efforts. Unlike most other advocacy groups, NAS and its Board have continued to support and stress the importance of independent research and analysis to inform public policy. Indeed, both NAS and its Board have used the findings and implications from RAND's ongoing evaluation to improve the initiative.

We are also grateful to the teachers and principals in the schools who gave of their time to respond to our questions, the staff in districts and states who helped us piece together relevant data, and the design teams who clarified issues along the way. All played a crucial role in providing information to better understand what kinds of schools the NAS designs are working with, and we appreciate their efforts and dedication to improving the capacity of schools, the professional development of teachers, and the well-being of students.

We thank the members of the Research Advisory Panel (funded by the Annenberg Foundation), who provide critical guidance to RAND's research on NAS. Members include Barbara Cervone, Paul

Hill, Janice Petrovich, Andrew Porter, Karen Sheingold, and Carol Weiss. We continue to learn from their experience, expertise, and encouragement. In addition, we are grateful to Tom Corcoran, Adam Gamoran, and Fred Newmann, who shared their expertise during the development of our principal and teacher surveys.

Several colleagues within RAND also contributed to the research underlying this report. Susan Bodilly, Co-Principal Investigator on this project with Mark Berends has been intimately involved in this research throughout. Daniel McCaffrey, of the RAND Statistics Group, provided invaluable advice on multilevel modeling. Thomas Glennan, senior adviser to this project, also provided helpful insights along the way. Joanna Heilbrunn was responsible for managing the principal phone interviews and administration of the teacher surveys that form the foundation of this report.

Despite the cooperation, support, and guidance of these individuals and agencies, any errors in this report remain our own.

Chapter One

AN OVERVIEW OF NEW AMERICAN SCHOOLS AND PURPOSE OF CURRENT REPORT

With high expectations, New American Schools (NAS) launched its efforts for whole-school reform in 1991. In an ambitious attempt to overcome the piecemeal approach to school reform that had largely proven ineffective, NAS aimed to develop, support, and disseminate "break the mold" school designs across the nation. As a private nonprofit organization, NAS's mission is to help schools and districts significantly raise the achievement of large numbers of students with both whole-school designs and the assistance that design teams provide during the implementation process.

This initiative is based on the premise that high-quality schools are established with external providers (design teams) providing assistance to schools for implementing designs:

> A Design Team is an organization that provides high-quality, focused, ongoing professional development for teachers and administrators organized around a meaningful and compelling vision of what students should know and be able to do. The vision, or design, offers schools a focus for their improvement efforts, along with guidance in identifying what students need to know and be able to do and how to get there. (New American Schools Development Corporation, 1997, p. 6.)

Glennan (1998, p. 11) describes a design further saying that it "articulates the school's vision, mission, and goals; guides the instructional program of the school; shapes the selection and socialization of the staff; and establishes common expectations for performance, behavior, and accountability among students, teachers, and parents."

NAS is currently in the scale-up phase of its effort in which the designs are being widely diffused in partnering jurisdictions across the nation. NAS's strategy for scale-up was based on the belief that school transformation could only take place with strong district support. At the beginning of the scale-up phase, NAS sought to partner with jurisdictions that would commit to five-year partnerships with NAS and the design teams to create a supportive environment for schoolwide reform. At the beginning of its scale-up phase in 1995, NAS partnered with ten jurisdictions: Cincinnati, Dade, several districts in Kentucky, Maryland, Memphis, Pittsburgh, Philadelphia, San Antonio, San Diego, and several districts in Washington State. All of these jurisdictions insisted that the participating schools meet district or state standards and that students be assessed against district and state mandated tests.

As NAS entered the scale-up phase, there were seven design teams:

- Audrey Cohen College [AC] (currently renamed Purpose-Centered Education);

- Authentic Teaching, Learning, and Assessment for All Students [AT];

- Co-NECT Schools [CON];

- Expeditionary Learning Outward Bound [EL];

- Modern Red Schoolhouse [MRSH];

- National Alliance for Restructuring Education [NARE] (currently renamed America's Choice Design Network); and

- Roots & Wings [RW].

While each design has unique features, the designs tend to emphasize school change in the following areas: organization and governance; teacher professional development; content and performance standards; curriculum and instructional strategies; and parent and community involvement.

The purposes and approaches of NAS and its design teams are the same as those for "schoolwide" Title I programs[1] and the Comprehensive School Reform Demonstration (CSRD) program also known as Obey-Porter.[2]

These two programs are targeted to improve performance of high-poverty schools. Each intends to improve student and school performance of low-performing schools through schools adopting a unified, coherent approach rather than adding fragmented programs or investing in personnel dedicated to a small group of students in pullout programs. Each intends to serve all students, not just subgroups of students. Thus, findings on NAS and its attempts at whole-school change can help inform the need for policy improvement for the many schools serving low-income students through the Title I and the CSRD programs.

LONGITUDINAL EVALUATION OF SCALE-UP OF NAS DESIGNS

Since its establishment in 1991, NAS contracted with RAND to provide analytical support. In 1995, RAND began an evaluation of the

---

[1] "Schoolwide" programs, available for funding since 1988, allow schools to use Title I money with other dollars to improve school performance as opposed to targeting Title I money solely to qualified students. The 1994 Improving America's Schools Act encourages more wide-range adoption of schoolwide programs (see American Association of School Administrators, 1995; http://www.ed.gov/legislation/ESEA). Currently, schools can use their Title I funding to improve the entire instructional program throughout the school if at least 50 percent of the students within the school are from poor families. (For a discussion of the 1994 Improving America's Schools Act, see U.S. Department of Education, 1993; and Borman et al., 1996).

[2] To further the implementation of comprehensive, whole-school reforms, the Comprehensive School Reform Demonstration program (CSRD), also known as Obey-Porter, was established in November 1997. These appropriations committed $145 million to be used to help schools develop comprehensive school reform based on reliable research and effective practices. The majority (83 percent in FY98 and 77 percent in FY99) of the funds are committed to Title I schools. Part of the money ($25 million in FY98 and FY99) was available to all public schools, including those ineligible for Title I, as part of the Fund for the Improvement in Education (FIE) program. Approximately 1,800 schools will receive at least $50,000 per year for three years under the CSRD program, beginning in FY98. There was an increase of $75 million for FY00 ($50 million in Title I/Section 1502 funds and $25 million in FIE funds) over the $145 million appropriated for FY98 and FY99, which will allow 1,000 additional schools to undertake comprehensive reform (see Kirby, Berends, et al., in review; http://www.ed.gov/offices/OESE/compreform).

scale-up of NAS designs to many schools. This longitudinal evaluation of the scale-up phase covers years 1995 to 2000 and addresses three major questions:

- What is the level of implementation in NAS schools?
- What impedes or facilitates that implementation?
- Does the adoption of NAS designs result in any changes to student and school outcomes?

Over this time period, RAND's program of studies has included:

- A longitudinal sample of over 100 NAS schools that began implementing early on in the scale-up phase, for which data on implementation and performance were gathered from principals, teachers, and districts (Berends, Kirby, et al., 2001);[3]
- Case studies in 40 schools to analyze implementation and the role that districts play in impeding or enabling comprehensive school reform (Bodilly, 1998);
- A description of how designs have evolved from the initial proposal stage to implementing at scale in real schools across the nation (Bodilly, 2001);
- Analyses in one urban school district of how designs promote changes in classroom instruction, teaching, and learning, and individual-level student achievement scores (Berends, Stockly, and Briggs, forthcoming);
- A case study analysis of what factors contribute to performance differences in high-implementing NAS sites; and
- Ongoing discussions with NAS staff and design team leaders.

---

[3]In addition, because the longitudinal sample focused on early-implementing schools, RAND collected data from a freshened sample of schools that began implementing NAS designs after 1995–1996. However, only four jurisdictions—Cincinnati, Memphis, San Antonio, and Washington—agreed to participate in this data collection effort, and 46 schools in these jurisdictions responded to the principal and teacher surveys. Although we analyzed data from these schools, the analyses did not change the results from those reported here substantially. Thus, these schools are not included in this report.

The original group of schools selected for the longitudinal study consisted of those schools initiating implementation of NAS designs in eight jurisdictions that NAS named as its partners during scale-up in either 1995–1996 or 1996–1997. These eight jurisdictions include: Cincinnati, Dade, Kentucky, Memphis, Philadelphia, Pittsburgh, San Antonio, and Washington State.[4] These jurisdictions reflect a range of support for implementation—from relatively supportive to no support at all (see Bodily, 1998).

At the beginning of scale-up, there were 184 schools that were implementing the NAS designs in these jurisdictions. These schools were the focus of the longitudinal evaluation, although the final sample of schools analyzed was smaller than this because of nonresponse, panel attrition, and schools dropping the designs.

A variety of data was collected to monitor the progress in implementation and performance in the NAS sites: (a) teacher surveys administered to all the teachers in the NAS schools; (b) principal phone interviews that took about an hour each to complete; (c) data provided by districts on school performance indicators (e.g., mandated test scores, attendance rates, promotion and drop out rates, and school demographic characteristics), and (d) site visits to schools and school districts to gather information through interviews and focus groups about district and school administrators' and teachers' reports of the progress of the NAS initiative.

Survey data were collected in 1997, 1998, and 1999, and provide information two, three, and four years after the scale-up. In addition, in 1999, schools that had dropped the design in either 1998 or 1999 were surveyed regarding the reasons for the decision. About 30 schools responded.[5]

---

[4]At the time we decided on the longitudinal sample of schools, Maryland and San Diego were not far enough along in their implementation to warrant inclusion in RAND's planned data collection efforts. Since then, several of the design teams report that they are implementing in Maryland and San Diego.

[5]It is difficult to calculate an attrition rate (i.e., schools that dropped the design as a percentage of the total sample) for the sample as a whole. Some schools that did not respond may well have dropped the design. Out of the 184 schools at the beginning of scale-up and excluding the 12 Pittsburgh schools that were later dropped from the study, at least 41 out of 172 schools had dropped the design, giving us a lower-bound attrition rate of approximately 24 percent.

As mentioned above, these quantitative data were complemented by interviews of key decisionmakers in the different jurisdictions undertaken in 1997 through 1999 to gather information about district-level policy changes and their effects on NAS implementation and outcomes. Incorporating the interview and focus group information provides a richer description of what has happened in the NAS schools and districts.

PURPOSE OF CURRENT REPORT

This report is one of two reports following the progress of schools in the longitudinal sample. The first report (Berends, Kirby, et al., 2001) analyzed implementation and performance in this group of schools three years after scale-up. This report is a follow-on to the earlier report, and provides a longitudinal (and final) look at the progress in implementation of designs four years after scale-up.

In particular, we address the following sets of research questions:

1. What is the mean level of implementation of NAS designs across this set of early implementing NAS schools four years after scale-up? Has implementation increased over time? Does implementation differ by jurisdiction and design team?

2. Has implementation deepened over time across schools, as measured by the change in the within-school and between-school variance of reported implementation levels?

3. What are the factors—in terms of teacher, school, design team, and district characteristics—that help explain the variation in implementation across schools and jurisdictions?

4. Among schools that dropped the NAS designs and for which we have data, what factors contributed to this decision?

The analyses that follow focus solely on schools that were part of NAS's strategy to build partnerships with districts to diffuse the designs to a large number of schools (i.e., scale-up). What follows, then, is a report on NAS's scale-up strategy. It is not a report on individual design teams' efforts. The designs have been implemented across the nation in many other schools than those examined here. While we present some comparisons among designs, we are more interested in understanding the progress in implementation within the jurisdictions that partnered with NAS at the beginning of the scale-up phase. Understanding how district, design team, school, and teacher factors contribute to implementation and early performance trends provides important lessons for comprehensive school reform efforts across the nation.

LIMITATIONS OF THE STUDY

It is important to understand the limitations of our sample and findings drawn from analyses of this sample of schools. For many of the design teams, these were the first schools to which they had provided assistance with implementing their designs on a fee-for-service basis. In addition, at the beginning of scale-up in 1995 most of the design teams reported to RAND that their designs were still unfinished. As a result, the early years of implementation on which we report saw many changes in both the designs and the assistance provided as the teams and the schools gained experience.

The strategy that NAS developed for scale-up (New American Schools Development Corporation, 1997) focused on a small number of jurisdictions that persuaded NAS that they possessed what NAS called supportive operating environments in which the designs could be implemented. In fact, for the most part these districts did not possess such environments. They had limited understanding of whole-school reform and the sort of design-based assistance that NAS design teams were intending to provide. The districts, NAS, and the design teams collectively and individually invented procedures and policies for design teams and the assistance they provided as the implementation unfolded. For example, districts varied widely in the processes set up for matching schools and designs, the contracts set up with designs, the services to be acquired, and the ways they monitored implementation of the designs (Bodily and Berends, 1999; Bodily, 1998).

In short, the early years of scale-up continued to be a time of uncertainty. There was some chaos and a great deal to be learned on the part of NAS, designs, districts, and schools. Thus, this report documents experiences that may differ from those of schools beginning implementation today. NAS and the design teams might have matured in large part because of the lessons learned about the ways in which jurisdictions, design teams, and schools must work together (Bodilly and Berends, 1999; Bodilly, 1998).

While the fact that designs were evolving over time as they gained experience and adapted to local contexts makes a longitudinal evaluation difficult, we believe that the information obtained in following these schools still offers valuable lessons, particularly for CSRD schools adopting a variety of school-reform models in many differing environments.

Thus, when interpreting the findings in this report, it is important to keep in mind these features of the population of schools we have studied.

ORGANIZATION OF THE REPORT

This report provides an update of the earlier study (Berends, Kirby, et al., 2001). The conceptual framework that forms the underpinning for the analyses in the earlier report as well as the current report is discussed in Chapter Two. Chapter Three provides details of the RAND longitudinal sample of NAS schools, and presents a brief description of these schools in terms of their demographic and school climate characteristics. Chapter Four presents an analysis, by jurisdiction and design team, of two summary implementation indicators. These implementation indicators are then analyzed in Chapter Five using multivariate models to tease out the net effect of various teacher, school, and implementation factors, controlling for other variables. Chapter Six provides a brief overview of findings from the exit interviews conducted with principals of 30 schools that reported dropping the design. Chapter Seven summarizes the results and their policy implications.

The appendixes provide additional detail regarding the core elements of designs and the derivation of the longitudinal analysis sample.

The analyses in this report offer both useful and provocative insights that will help inform the NAS effort and larger federal efforts to implement comprehensive school reform in low-performing schools.

Chapter Two

CONCEPTUAL FRAMEWORK FOR ANALYZING IMPLEMENTATION IN NEW AMERICAN SCHOOLS

NAS's mission is to help schools and districts significantly raise the achievement of large numbers of students with design-based assistance (New American Schools Development Corporation, 1999). In fact, improving student and school performance is a critical goal of all comprehensive school reforms.

CORE ELEMENTS OF DESIGNS

To accomplish the goal of improving performance, each design team has a "theory of action" that establishes a link between elements of the design and student performance. The NAS designs range from relatively specific descriptions of how schools should be organized and what materials and professional development should be relied on to less-specific visions and processes for school restructuring.

One of the more specific NAS designs is RW, which builds on years of research and implementation experiences with the reading and writing program *Success for All*. RW provides an abundance of print materials, assessments, professional development, and specified organizational changes (e.g., homogeneous instructional groups that are reorganized frequently to address students' needs). The design begins implementation with a specific focus on changing curriculum and instruction.

In contrast, some of the other NAS designs are more process oriented. For instance, EL is less structured than RW and is based on design principles that reflect the design's origins in the Outward

Bound program. Students' experiences in EL schools consist primarily of engaging in multidisciplinary, project-based learning expeditions that include intellectual, service, and physical dimensions. Teachers play a critical role in developing the expeditions, which involves a great deal of effort and imagination.

Thus, it is important to remember the unique attributes of each design in terms of the components of schooling emphasized, the different strategies for implementation, and the complexity and specificity of the design. Certainly we cannot capture all of the uniqueness of each design in the current report, but RAND's other studies of NAS have pointed to these characteristics and the importance of looking at changes in the designs over time (see Bodilly, 2001; Berends, 1999; Glennan, 1998).

While each design is unique, they all tend to emphasize five core components:

- organization and governance;
- professional life of teachers;
- content and performance expectations;
- curriculum and instructional strategies; and
- parent and community involvement.

Appendix A describes each of these components in more detail. Teacher-reported indicators of these core elements are used to create a core implementation index, the dependent variable in our analyses.

FACTORS AFFECTING IMPLEMENTATION

The process of school change to improve student achievement is complex and difficult. It requires the coordination of a variety of actors and factors to make it work. As Datnow and Stringfield (2000: 199) write:

> [R]eform adoption, implementation, and sustainability, and school change more generally, are not processes that result from individuals or institutions acting in isolation from one another. Rather, they

are the result of the interrelations between and across groups in different contexts, at various points in time. In this way, forces at the state and district levels, at the design team level, and at the school and classroom levels shape the way in which reforms fail or succeed.

Based on an extensive literature review, Fullan (2001) groups the factors affecting implementation into three main categories:

(a) **Characteristics of the change itself,** in terms of need and relevance of the change, clarity, complexity, and quality and practicality of the program;

(b) **Local factors,** that capture "the social conditions of change; the organization or setting in which people work; and the planned and unplanned events and activities that influence whether or not given change attempts will be productive." (Fullan, 2001: 80). These include characteristics of teachers, principals, communities, and districts; and

(c) **Factors external to the local system,** such as role of government agencies, other outsiders, and external assistance.

We draw and expand on these factors to highlight the role of each when assessing NAS's whole-school reform initiative, although we group them in slightly different ways. The framework portrayed in Figure 2.1 is an attempt to capture the complex "system of variables" (Fullan, 2001: 71) that is at the heart of educational change.

Teacher Background

Without willing and able teachers who embrace reform and provide the necessary leadership, no reform can be enacted, no matter how effective it may be. Teachers are the "street-level bureaucrats" at the core of educational change (Weatherly and Lipsky, 1977) and as Fullan succinctly stated, educational change depends on "what teachers do and think—it's as simple and as complex as that" (Fullan, 1991, p. 117).

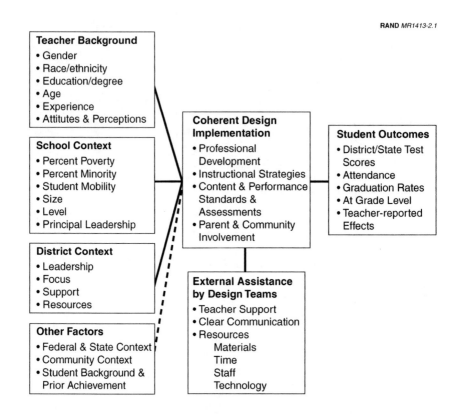

Figure 2.1—A Conceptual Framework for Analyzing Progress and
Performance in NAS Schools

Educators must respond to multiple, simultaneous pressures and demands. For many teachers, policy goals and activities are simply part of a broader environment that presses in upon their classrooms. Their ability to cope with these demands, and their commitment to change are crucial to coherent and sustained implementation. For as Tyack and Cuban (1995) state, teachers often implement new reform programs with "pedagogical pasts" (see also Hargreaves, 1994; McLaughlin et al., 1990; Muncey and McQuillan, 1996).

Moreover, engagement in reforms may be affected by teachers' personal characteristics, such as their age and experience (Huberman, 1989), gender (Datnow, 1998, 2000a), and race (Foster, 1993; Bascia,

2000), but not necessarily correlated (Berends, 2000; Datnow and Castellano, 2000), so it remains important to examine these characteristics for the specific reforms under consideration.

Thus, teachers matter: their experience, subject-based expertise, attitudes, and orientations, (and characteristics that may affect those attitudes such as age, gender, race/ethnicity) are important in determining the degree and level of implementation.

Fullan's theory of educational change highlights the importance of working relationships among teachers in implementation of change: collegiality, open communication, trust, support, learning on the job, and morale are closely interrelated (Fullan, 2001; Rosenholtz, 1989). Newmann and colleagues show a strong link between professional learning community, teacher learning, and student performance (Newmann and Wehlage, 1995).

In short, teachers are central to any organizational changes that might alter student-teacher interactions occurring in classrooms to improve student learning (Gamoran et al., 1995; Oakes et al., 1992). Over time, teachers carry with them a great deal of knowledge based on their educational attainment, teaching experience, and other personal characteristics that together are likely to be related to their engagement in schoolwide restructuring activities (Louis and Marks, 1998). Thus, it is important to examine the relationships among various teacher background characteristics, design implementation, and reported effects of schoolwide designs on teachers and students.

School Characteristics

Clearly, schools matter: their leadership, environment, and climate.

Research has consistently shown that the principal strongly influences the likelihood of change (Fullan, 1991, 2001; Berends, Kirby, et al., 2001; McLaughlin and Talbert, 2001; Newmann et al., 2000; Day et al., 2000; Bryk et al., 1998a; Berman and McLaughlin, 1978). As Fullan writes:

> I know of no improving school that doesn't have a principal who is good at leading improvement. (2001: 141.)

However, there is general consensus that direct principal influence is by itself not a powerful influence on change; rather principals "facilitate" the process of change. For example, leadership of the principal may translate into the ability to obtain sufficient resources for the school and support teachers in their efforts to implement change. Elmore, for example, writes:

> [T]he job of administrative leaders is primarily about enhancing the skills and knowledge of people in the organization, creating a common culture of expectations around the use of those skills and knowledge, holding the various pieces of the organization together in a productive relationship with each other, and holding individuals accountable for their contributions to the collective result. (2000: 15.)

Characteristics of schools are also likely to influence the adoption of schoolwide designs and their effects on student learning. In our work, we are examining whether schools' "structural" characteristics such as the minority and socioeconomic composition of the school, school size, and school level (elementary, middle, high school) are related to implementation and performance (Berends, 1999).

Schools that face challenges in terms of poverty may encounter difficulties with restructuring efforts such as whole-school designs because high-poverty schools may lack the necessary resources to provide a quality education (Lippman et al., 1996) because students may have lower levels of engagement, effort, and aspirations (Hoffer, 1992; Ralph, 1990; Fordham and Ogbu, 1987), and because teachers may not have the necessary supports they need to foster collaborative relationships necessary for school improvement efforts (Hoffer, 1992; see also Berends, Kirby, et al., 2001; Berends and King, 1994).

Yet, because federal funding such as Title I is oriented toward disadvantaged students and schools, the effects of socioeconomic and minority composition are likely to be mediated by the effect of increased resources. In fact, since the 1994 reauthorization of Title I, schools with more than half of their students eligible for free or reduced price lunch may use Title I funds for schoolwide programs. Thus, there may be a positive relationship between high-poverty schools and schoolwide implementations such as NAS designs because of such funding sources.

Other school structural factors (size and level) may inhibit school-wide implementation of reforms. For example, larger secondary schools are more complex organizations and are likely to resist organizational change (Perrow, 1986). Moreover, larger schools may be characterized as more bureaucratic in organization rather than communitarian, resulting in a climate where teachers are less likely to collaborate around a common mission and vision as envisioned by whole-school designs (see Lee, Bryk, and Smith, 1993; Lee and Smith, 1995, 1997). For example, Newmann, Rutter, and Smith (1989) found that teachers were more likely to report a communal atmosphere (e.g., teachers as colleagues who share beliefs and values, teachers can count on other staff members to help, and cooperative efforts among staff) in smaller schools than larger ones (see also Bryk and Driscoll, 1988).

District Factors

Research also underscores the importance of the external environment, especially district support and stability of leadership, in the process of change (Bodily and Berends, 1999; Bodily, 1998; Glennan, 1998; Fullan, 1991). The district can facilitate and foster change by providing resources for the school and for professional staff development, and showing active support for schools implementing designs.

Datnow and Stringfield, in their comprehensive, longitudinal study of 300 schools implementing a variety of reforms for at-risk students report:

> We found that clear, strong district support positively impacted reform implementation, and that lack thereof often negatively impacted implementation . . . schools that sustained reforms had district and state allies that protected reform efforts during periods of transition or crisis and secured resources (money, time, staff, and space) essential to reforms. (2000: 194–195.)

In RAND's work on NAS, Bodily (1998) found that districts played a strong role in determining the initial and sustained viability of the relationship between the school and the design team. Early on in the scale-up phase, many schools' staff members had complaints about the district's poor planning and providing too little time for making decisions, issues brought up in other assessments of the adoption of schoolwide programs (Wong and Meyer, 1998).

RAND's prior case studies (see Bodilly, 1998; Bodilly and Berends, 1999) revealed that higher average levels of implementation were found in districts that had a stable district leadership that placed a high priority on the effort, that lacked a major budget crisis or other crisis, and that had a history of trust between the central office and the schools. School-level respondents directly linked these factors to greater efforts at implementation. When these factors were missing, school respondents reported that their own efforts stalled or were less intense.

Moreover, crucial central office political support and attention can be buttressed by significant changes in regulatory and financial practices. Schools attempting comprehensive school reform to address their particular problems can be supported through increased site-level control over their curriculum and instruction, their budgets, their positions and staffing, and most essentially their mission. Comprehensive school reform is not confined to the adoption of a new mandated curriculum or a few new instructional strategies. Instead, it requires rethinking and adoption at the school-level of new curriculum and instructional approaches and the accompanying professional development. District flexibility in allowing schools to pursue this rethinking is a critical aspect for design-based schools. Development and implementation of such curriculum and instructional strategies at the school level may be significantly hampered without district support through resource allocation for instructional positions, materials, technology, professional development, etc.

Many schools are on innovation overload; they are suffering the burden "of having a torrent of unwanted, uncoordinated policies and innovations raining down on them from hierarchical bureaucracies" (Fullan, 2001: 22). In a recent survey of schools in districts in California and Texas, Hatch (2000) reported that two-thirds of the schools were working with three or more improvement programs; over one-fifth were working with six or more; and in one district, close to one-fifth of the schools were working with nine or more programs simultaneously. Districts can make a world of difference in protecting schools from such overload and fragmentation.

In short, district-level politics, policies, and practices may promote or derail schoolwide reform efforts such as the NAS designs.

External Assistance by Design Teams

How schools go about selecting a design has implications for the implementation that follows (Bodilly, 1998; Datnow, 2000b; Desimone, 2000; Consortium for Policy Research in Education, 1998; Smith et al., 1998; Stringfield, 1998; Ross et al., 1997). For example, if a school is forced to adopt a design, it is not surprising that teachers would resist engaging in the activities of the design. Yet, some schools are often targets for forced restructuring efforts, particularly those that exhibit chronic poor performance. Thus, a critical aim of the NAS designs before implementation even begins is to obtain the buy-in of teachers for the planned restructuring activities. Most of the designs require between 75 and 80 percent of the teachers voting in favor of the designs. The rationale is that if the vast majority of the staff vote to adopt the design, they will commit to making the changes necessary during the implementation process. However, Datnow and Stringfield (2000), in their review of innovative programs found that even when there is the requirement of teacher "buy-in," agreement can be superficial:

> In several of our studies we found that educators adopted reform models without thinking through how the model would suit their school's goals, culture, teachers or students . . . even when opportunities to gather information were available, educators seldom made well-informed choices about reform designs. . . . (2000: 191; see also Hatch, 2000.)

Therefore, we measure extent of teacher support for the design, in addition to whether teachers voted to adopt the model.

Clear communication by designs to schools is critical for not only the selection of the design, but implementation of it—something that external assistance providers have found challenging when attempting to help a large number of schools (Bodilly, 1998). This goes back to Fullan's earlier point about clarity of the change as a factor affecting implementation; the more complex the reform, the greater the need for clarity. At the same time, Fullan (2001) warns against what he refers to as "false clarity" in which teachers interpret the change in an oversimplified way. For example, Stigler and Hiebert (1999) in their video analysis of Grade 8 mathematics lessons showed that teachers introducing reforms in a superficial manner actually made matters worse.

Communication to schools both in the selection and implementation process can take several different forms, including design fairs, print materials, use of computer software and the Internet, workshops, retreats, school visits, and site-based facilitators. For instance, school visits by design team staff on a regular basis to help teachers address issues related to developing curriculum units or the use of rubrics to assess students are intended to help teachers implement project-based learning and the assessment of that learning within the context of the design. Other types of communication might be effective as well, and the clearer and more consistent the information provided about implementation by designs to schools, the smoother the implementation process is likely to be.

Another characteristic of the change that is important in implementation is the quality and practicality of the program. Large-scale change requires attention to high-quality teaching and training materials. In addition, for implementation of any program, resources to support implementation and professional development are critical (Keltner, 1998; McLaughlin, 1990). It is a common finding that when resources decrease or disappear, the implementation is likely to diminish (Glennan, 1998; Montjoy and O'Toole, 1979). If teachers receive the needed funds, professional development from design teams for design implementation, materials to support implementation, and time to plan and develop the program, it is likely that implementation will deepen over time.

Other Factors

Those who have studied implementation of educational programs have pointed to other factors that affect implementation such as the federal and/or state policy environment, the larger community context including parent support for school change, and student background and prior achievement (e.g., Elmore and Rothman, 1999; Berends, Grissmer, Kirby, and Williamson, 1999; Grissmer and Flanagan, 1998; Fullan, 1991, 2001).

The federal and state policy context is likely to play an important role in implementing schoolwide reform (see Fullan, 1991, 2001; Koretz and Barron, 1998).

> If we are to achieve large-scale reform, governments are essential. They have the potential to be a major force for transformation. The historical evidence to date, however, suggests that few governments have gotten this right. (Fullan, 2001: 220.)

Governments have followed three separate strands of activities: pushing accountability, providing incentives (pressure and support), and fostering capacity-building. Most governments have placed great emphasis on the first; some have successfully combined the first two, but few, until recently, have paid attention to capacity-building (Fullan, 2001). Darling-Hammond (2000) in her review of state policies concluded that the states that invested in capacity-building (in terms of investments in teacher knowledge, training, and skills) have been more successful in raising student achievement. The Education Commission of the States (1999) in drawing together lessons learned from implementing whole-school reform pointed out that support from the state education department is key for long-term success.

The recent CSRD program is another federal effort at fostering capacity-building. The program directly supports design-based reforms such as NAS by providing at least $50,000 to schools to pay for the related services. Some states and districts with high-stakes accountability systems are strongly encouraging or forcing low-performing schools to adopt designs (see Kirby, Berends, Naftel, and Sloan, in review) as a means of improvement. They may also facilitate a more effective matching process for schools to select designs based on their local needs by helping schools with needs assessments, providing additional information, and negotiations with model developers (see Bodilly and Berends, 1999; Bodilly, 1998; Smith et al., 1996).

An important limitation of most government initiatives is that governments emphasize "adoption," not implementation. Elmore (2000) points out that many government policies "are quintessential structural changes in that they imply absolutely nothing about either the content or quality of instruction" (2000: 10). It is important for governments to realize the long timeline needed for implementation and to stay in for the long haul by being willing to invest in the long-term.

The support of the larger community and parents is likely to affect implementation as well (Fullan, 1991). Parent and community demand for reform, their readiness for it, and their ongoing support of it have important ramifications for implementation. One of the main obstacles to implementing a variety of restructuring efforts vis-à-vis the educational bureaucracy may be that many community members do not see the need for change (Berends and King, 1994; see also Jennings, 1996, 1998).

An additional set of factors that affect implementation of school restructuring efforts and their effects is student background and prior achievement (Berends et al., 1999; Koretz, 1996; Meyer, 1996). While policymakers focus on the "lever" at the school level to manipulate to improve learning opportunities and performance, several studies have shown the importance of student background in the learning process (see Coleman et al., 1966; Jencks et al., 1972; Gamoran, 1987, 1992; Bryk, Lee, and Holland, 1993).

While we understand the importance of these "other" factors, the analyses that follow are of more direct measures of the factors in the boxes in Figure 2.1 with solid lines between them.

This chapter has described the theoretical framework that underpins the analyses of implementation reported here. We now turn to a description of the longitudinal sample of NAS schools that forms the database for our study.

Chapter Three

LONGITUDINAL SAMPLE OF NEW AMERICAN SCHOOLS

DEFINING THE ANALYSIS SAMPLE

Of the 184 schools identified as the universe for the study in 1997, we completed interviews with 155 principals. However, 25 of the 155 schools (about 15 percent) reported that they were in an exploratory year or a planning year with implementation expected in the future. Because our interest is in understanding the specific activities that were occurring within schools that were implementing a NAS design to some extent, we limited our analysis sample to the 130 schools that reported they were implementing a NAS design.[1]

In the spring of 1998, all 184 schools were once again surveyed. The completed sample size of implementing schools consisted of 142 schools. However, the overlap between the 1997 and 1998 samples was incomplete. For purposes of the longitudinal analysis we limited the analysis sample to schools that met two criteria:

- Schools were implementing in both 1997 and 1998; and,

- Schools had complete data (i.e., from teachers and principals) in both years.

---

[1]These were schools that had complete principal data and at least five teachers responding to the teacher surveys. For more details regarding the population of schools and the derivation of the longitudinal sample, see Appendix B.

Of the 130 schools implementing in 1997 for which we had complete data, nine had either dropped the design or had reverted to planning, and another 17 had missing or incomplete data. Thus, the final sample for the analysis used by the earlier study (Berends, Kirby, et al., 2001), consisted of 104 schools across seven jurisdictions. All 104 schools had been implementing at least two years. The distribution of these 104 schools by jurisdiction and by design team is shown in Table 3.1.

As of spring 1998, 40 percent of the 104 schools reported two years of implementation, 35 percent of the schools reported three years of implementation, and 25 percent of schools reported four years or more of implementation. More than half of the NARE schools reported four or more years of implementation.

The various criteria we used to define the sample all bias the sample to some extent in a positive direction in terms of expected implementation. RAND's sample of NAS sites is drawn initially from a set of NAS schools that expressed interest in implementing designs in districts that had formed a partnership with NAS. In addition, we chose schools where principals reported that they had been implementing the designs either partly or wholly for at least two years in 1998. This was done to ensure some degree of comparability across schools in terms of where they were in implementing designs. But, omitting schools that reported they were not implementing or had just started implementing in 1998 from the sample makes our

Table 3.1

**Analysis Sample: Schools That Were Implementing in Both
1997 and 1998, with Complete Data in Both Years**

Jurisdiction	AC	AT	CON	EL	MRSH	NARE	RW	Total
				Design Team				
Cincinnati			5	5			6	16
Dade	1		2				1	4
Kentucky						20		20
Memphis	4	4	5	5	3		8	29
Philadelphia		6			1			7
San Antonio				6	3			9
Washington		7				12		19
Total	5	17	12	16	7	32	15	104

analysis relatively more likely to find effects of designs on teaching and student achievement, where they exist.

The Longitudinal Sample for the Current Study

All schools that reported some degree of implementation in 1998 were surveyed again in the spring of 1999. Among the 104 schools that formed the longitudinal sample for the earlier study, we obtained complete data on 71 schools, i.e., from principals and at least five teachers in the school. Principals in 10 of the 104 schools reported that they had dropped the design but the attrition in the sample was largely due to nonresponse (13 schools were missing principal data as well as some teacher data; 10 schools had fewer than five teachers responding to the survey). Table 3.2 compares respondents with nonrespondents. In terms of jurisdictions, nonresponse was higher among schools in Washington state, Cincinnati, and Kentucky; in terms of design teams, nonresponse was higher in CON, EL, and NARE schools. Schools that had been implementing for three and five or more years in 1998 were disproportionately represented among the nonrespondents. Nonresponding schools tended to be less poor than responding schools, and to have lower proportions of minority students. However, these schools reported fairly similar levels of overall implementation of NAS designs as the responding schools and the within-school variability in reported implementation was the same. Despite the high attrition and somewhat differing characteristics of the nonrespondents, the patterns of implementation we find here are remarkably similar to the findings of the earlier study (Berends, Kirby, et al., 2001) based on the 104 schools.

The distribution of the 71 schools in the longitudinal sample by jurisdictions and design team is shown in Table 3.3. In the longitudinal sample, a little over a quarter of the schools are NARE schools that are primarily located in Kentucky, while AT, RW, and EL each account for 15–18 percent of the sample. AC, CON, and MRSH have the smallest number of schools in the longitudinal sample.

All 71 schools had been implementing for three or more years by 1999. About 44 percent of the sample had been implementing for three years; a little over 30 percent for four years; and the remaining one-fourth of the sample for five years or more (most of these were NARE schools).

Table 3.2

**A Comparison of Respondents and Nonrespondents in the
Longitudinal Sample in 1999, Based on 1998 Data**

Selected Characteristics	Nonrespondents	Respondents
	Number of Schools	
Jurisdiction		
Cincinnati	6	10
Dade	3	1
Kentucky	7	13
Memphis	5	24
Philadelphia	1	6
San Antonio	2	7
Washington	9	10
Design team		
AC	1	4
AT	4	13
CON	6	6
EL	6	10
MRSH	0	7
NARE	13	19
RW	3	12
Years implementing in 1998		
2 years	11	31
3 years	13	22
4 years	4	13
≥5 years	5	5
	Percentage	
Elementary schools	60.6	66.2
Mean percent students eligible for free/reduced price lunch	58.5	66.3
Mean percent minority students	52.7	63.0
Total number of schools	33	71

Teacher Sample

The sample size of teachers who responded to the survey was approximately 1,700 in 1997, and 1,500 in both 1998 and 1999. The average response rate among teachers has fallen over time in the 71 schools, from 73 percent in 1997 to 59 percent in 1999. The interquartile range for response rates, representing the middle 50 percent of the distribution, was 41–75 percent. Response rates were generally lower in 1998 compared with 1997, but response rates in 1999 were comparable with those of 1998 in most jurisdictions.

Table 3.3

Distribution of the 1999 Longitudinal Sample, by Jurisdiction
and Design Team

| | Design Team | | | | | | | |
Jurisdiction	AC	AT	CON	EL	MRSH	NARE	RW	Total
Cincinnati			3	2			5	10
Dade	1							1
Kentucky						13		13
Memphis	3	4	3	4	3		7	24
Philadelphia		5			1			6
San Antonio				4	3			7
Washington		4				6		10
Total	4	13	6	10	7	19	12	71

OVERVIEW OF NAS SCHOOLS IN THE 1999 ANALYSIS SAMPLE

It is helpful to provide a broad overview of the schools in the analysis sample. Overall, NAS partnered with jurisdictions that were predominantly urban, high poverty, and high minority (Berends, 1999; Berends, Kirby, et al., 2001). Compared with the jurisdictions, most of the NAS designs were assisting schools with disproportionately high percentages of poor and minority students. NAS principals reported greater problems with absenteeism and school readiness when compared to the nation's principals (for details see Berends, 1999). Some of the design teams are in schools where the reported problems of readiness were more severe, such as RW and EL. School readiness included principal reports about problems such as students coming to school unprepared to learn, poor nutrition, poor student health, student apathy, and lack of academic challenge. By and large, school safety was not perceived by principals to be a greater problem in the NAS sites when compared to the nation's principals.

Table 3.4 shows selected school characteristics by jurisdiction for the longitudinal sample. The average poverty rate, defined as percentage of students eligible for free/reduced price lunch, in the sample was 66 percent, and 62 percent of the students being served by these schools were minority. Memphis and San Antonio schools had much

Table 3.4

Selected School Characteristics, by Jurisdiction

Jurisdiction	Free/Reduced Price Lunch	Minority	Mobility	LEP	No. of Schools
	Percentage				
Cincinnati	67.7	68.2	13.6	0.2	10
Dade	65.0	96.0	7.0	5.0	1
Kentucky	48.3	24.1	10.2	1.6	13
Memphis	81.9	90.2	19.6	1.2	24
Philadelphia	71.2	57.0	13.3	6.7	6
San Antonio	99.0	94.2	19.4	14.3	7
Washington	25.0	14.5	10.3	3.3	10
NAS average	66.3	62.0	15.1	3.1	71

higher proportions of poor and minority students. In addition, these schools were characterized by high student mobility in general.[2] San Antonio schools, not surprisingly, were serving a high proportion of limited English proficient (LEP) students.

In terms of design teams, MRSH and RW tended to be in the poorest schools, while AC and RW tended to be in the schools with the highest percentage of minority students. Nearly one in five students in RW and CON schools were likely to move during the academic school year.

This provides a context for our discussion of the progress of implementation in NAS schools that is the focus of the remainder of the report.

---

[2]Mobility rates are based on the following question in the principal survey: "On average, what percentage of your total student body enrolled at the beginning of the school year is still enrolled at the end of the school year?" Percentages in Table 3.4 are calculated as 100 minus this reported percentage.

Chapter Four

STATUS OF IMPLEMENTATION

This chapter addresses whether schools implemented critical components of the NAS designs. The earlier report (Berends, Kirby, et al., 2001) reported on the status of implementation of the NAS designs as of spring 1998; this report provides an update on the status of implementation a year later. As we showed earlier, by the spring of 1999, all of the schools in our longitudinal sample had been implementing for three or more years.

RESEARCH QUESTIONS

Our analyses focus on two sets of research questions:

1. **What is the mean level of implementation of NAS designs across this set of early implementing NAS schools three years after scale-up? Has implementation increased over time? Does implementation differ by jurisdiction and design team?** We should expect an increase in the mean level of implementation over time as implementation takes hold, but the rate of change in the level of implementation is likely to vary depending on whether schools are in the relatively early phase of implementation or are more experienced with the designs. For example, if—as seems likely—implementation follows a polynomial function, increasing sharply over the first few years and then leveling off, we would expect sharp increases in mean implementation in the first few years after adoption, as schools moved to adopt and deploy key components of the designs. After a few years, however, there should be a tailing off of the increases in mean implementation

levels, as designs become more schoolwide and more an integral part of the daily work life of principals, teachers, and students.

2. **Has implementation deepened over time both within and between schools, as measured by the change in the variance of reported implementation levels within and between schools?** As implementation deepens, we should expect a decrease in the variance of the implementation index both between and within schools, as designs become more schoolwide, and there is greater consensus, clarity, and coherence in what teachers within a school are doing. This latter effect will be tempered by jurisdictional effects because of the varying degrees of support from districts as well as changes in the designs themselves as they seek to adapt to local contexts. In this report, we focus largely on between-school variance.[1]

ORGANIZATION OF THE CHAPTER

The remainder of this chapter is divided into several sections.

- The next section provides details about the core implementation index we use to measure implementation;

- We then discuss the challenges inherent in measuring implementation within and across designs, given that each design is unique and that designs themselves may be evolving over time and adapting to local environments;

- The following section presents findings from our analyses of the index, using the longitudinal sample; and

- A final section provides a brief summary of the chapter.

---

[1]In analyses not reported here, we found that declines in the variability of reported implementation both within and between these schools were small between 1997 and 1998; however, in almost every case, the variance within school increased between 1998 and 1999. It was also true that the between-schools variance in implementation was much smaller than the within-school variance, and was generally stable over time, with a couple of exceptions. These analyses were conducted using a different index than the one reported here. Our reviewers suggested omitting these analyses from this report for reasons of clarity. For further details, see Berends, Kirby, et al., 2001.

CONSTRUCTING A CORE IMPLEMENTATION INDEX[2]

The core implementation index is a summative scale of teacher responses as to the degree to which the following described their school (on a scale of 1–6, with 1 = does not describe my school, and 6 = clearly describes my school):[3]

- Parents and community members are involved in the educational program;

- Student assessments are explicitly linked to academic standards;

- Teachers develop and monitor student progress with personalized, individualized learning programs;

- Student grouping is fluid, multiage, or multiyear;

- Teachers are continual learners and team members through professional development, common planning, and collaboration; and

- Performance expectations are made explicit to students so that they can track their progress over time.

We analyze this overall implementation measure for two reasons:

First, the core function of schools is teaching and learning. Therefore, we selected those teacher-reported implementation indicators that were related more directly to influencing what goes on in teachers' lives and inside classrooms. From an organizational perspective, classroom instruction is the core technology of school organizations

---

[2]In our earlier report, Berends, Kirby, et al. (2001), we also developed a design team–specific implementation index that measures implementation of both shared and some unique aspects of the designs. The design team–specific index allowed us to measure implementation of each design on components that are unique to and emphasized by the design. The shortcoming of this index is that it is not directly comparable across designs, because it varies both in terms of items and number of items included in the index. We also measured implementation in the current report using this index, but because the analyses did not add substantially to the conclusions, we do not show them here.

[3]The alpha reliability of this index was 0.81. The range of correlations for the individual items was from 0.21 to 0.57.

and the primary mechanism through which learning occurs (Gamoran et al., 1995; Gamoran and Dreeben, 1986; Parsons, 1959). It is this core function of schools that the designs ultimately want to influence and it is this aspect of implementation that our overall implementation index aims to measure.

Second, we want to examine factors related to implementation, and this summary measure allows us to present our results in a parsimonious manner.

MEASURING IMPLEMENTATION WITHIN AND ACROSS DESIGNS: SOME CAVEATS

As we discussed in our earlier work, measuring progress in implementation broadly across a wide set of schools in several partnering jurisdictions involved a number of challenges (Berends, Kirby, et al., 2001).

First, each design is unique. Attempting to develop a common set of indicators that measures implementation *across* designs is difficult, particularly when design teams adapt their programs to the local needs of the schools (Bodilly, 2001). However, despite their differences, design teams do aim to change some key conditions of schools in common ways, such as school organization, expectations for student performance, professional development, instructional strategies, and parent involvement.[4] We attempted to draw on these commonalities to guide the construction of an index that could be used to broadly measure "core" implementation across designs.

Second, the difficulties of constructing indices that capture the key components of a design are compounded by the fact that these design components may themselves be evolving (see Bodilly, 2001). For example, design teams may change their implementation strategies because of lessons learned during development and implementation experiences in various sites.

---

[4]With the recent support of the federal CSRD program, schools need to make sure that their plan covers these areas. If one particular design team or CSRD model does not cover these and several other areas of school improvement, then schools need to adopt more than one design or model (see Kirby, Berends, et al., in review).

Third, even if one developed measures on which there was general agreement that they fully captured the key facets of designs, the local context introduces a great deal of variability that must be taken into account (Bodily, 1998; Bodily and Berends, 1999). For example, while a design may focus on project-based learning over several weeks of the semester, this may be superseded by district-mandated curricula that take priority over significant portions of each school day.

Fourth, because the index is so general, it may be measuring more than just reform implementation.[5] Each of the components is a characteristic of effective schools, so schools may be pursuing these separately as school goals or as part of a district initiative. An increase in any one of these measures may not necessarily mean higher implementation of the model. For example, it may be that the design is helping the school to better attain these goals, or even that the school has been more successful in meeting these goals over time, independent of the model.

Fifth, it is important to note that all the results reported here on implementation are based on teachers' responses to surveys. The usefulness of what we can learn and infer from the analyses is heavily dependent on the quality of the data that are obtained from these surveys. In some instances, what we find has been validated by RAND's early case studies and other research (Bodily, 1998; Ross et al., 1997; Datnow and Stringfield, 1997; Stringfield and Datnow, 1998), but for some indicators, all we have are teacher-reported survey measures.

Sixth, in the analysis sample of NAS schools that we examine, small sample sizes for some design teams make traditional tests of statistical significance somewhat more difficult to apply. That is, with larger sample sizes, we would have more power to detect differences and effects. Thus, in the school-level descriptive analyses in this chapter, we focus on what appear to be educationally substantive differences where appropriate.

---

[5]We thank one of our reviewers, Amanda Datnow, for making this point.

Despite these challenges, as said earlier in Chapter 1, evaluation remains an important component of any effort to change schools, and it is important to develop and refine sets of indicators that are informative not only for researchers, but for design teams, educators, and policymakers.

Thus, in order to address our questions about implementation stated above, we developed the core implementation index described earlier to broadly measure implementation of the *major* shared components of the designs across the sites. The core implementation index is useful for understanding the progress of the NAS schools during the scale-up phase.

Our focus in this chapter is on variation in implementation both among jurisdictions as well as design teams, where appropriate. The small sample size for some designs, the widely differing environments facing designs implemented in different jurisdictions, and the varying degree of support from districts make comparisons of implementation across design teams somewhat problematic.

In what follows, the school is the unit of analysis. In some instances, we conduct multiple comparison tests of differences among means, but, as we mentioned earlier, small sample sizes mean that finding statistically significant differences is somewhat more difficult in these data.[6] In addition, outliers can make the means less representative than in more well-behaved distributions. These tests remain useful, however, in highlighting differences across jurisdictions and design teams that are both substantively and statistically meaningful. Nevertheless, our primary emphasis in this chapter is on the patterns that emerge from the analyses taken together rather than on particular differences for any given indicator.

---

[6]Statistically significant here refers to the mean differences being significant at the 0.05 probability level or less. This is based on the multiple comparison test using the Bonferonni correction. When conducting multiple tests, say n, and setting the critical level to α for each test, the chances of falsely rejecting *at least one* of the hypotheses is $1 - (1 - 0.05)^n$ if the tests are independent. The Bonferonni correction allows us to control for the fact that we are conducting multiple tests and to ensure that the overall chance of falsely rejecting each hypothesis remains α.

RESULTS: DIFFERENCES IN IMPLEMENTATION BY JURISDICTION AND DESIGN TEAM[7]

We began by analyzing differences in the mean implementation level in 1999 by jurisdiction and design team. We then focused on changes over time. In 1999, the mean implementation index was 4.32, with a standard deviation of 0.52. We calculated a standardized z-score for each jurisdiction and each design team, based on the 1999 mean and standard deviation for all schools.[8]

Differences in Implementation by Jurisdiction, 1999

Our earlier work had found large differences in the distribution of the core implementation index across the jurisdictions as well as design teams. Figures 4.1 and 4.2 show the distribution of this normalized index by jurisdiction and design team for 1999, when all schools had been implementing for three or more years. Kentucky and Memphis ranked relatively high on this index with means that were 0.60 and 0.33 of a standard deviation higher than the overall mean while Washington and San Antonio ranked the lowest, with means that were 0.77 and 0.87 of a standard deviation lower than the overall mean.[9] This ranking mirrors what we had found in 1998, with the exception that Philadelphia, which had ranked second lowest in terms of implementation, now ranks higher. Memphis schools also displayed the greatest spread in the data, as is evident from the long

---

[7]The first three graphs of this chapter are portrayed with box-and-whisker diagrams, which show the distribution of the particular indicator being examined. In a box-and-whisker diagram, the line in the box is at the median value—half the values fall above the line and half fall below. Each "box" captures the middle 50 percent of the distribution. The lines, called "whiskers," at each end of the box show the range of scores beyond the upper and lower quartiles. Outliers are indicated by the shaded circles. The box-and-whisker plot thus allows us to compare the centers (median or center of the box), spread (measured by the interquartile range or the height of the box), and tails of the different distributions.

[8]We thank our reviewer, Robert Croninger, for his suggestion that we use standardized metrics to make calculation of effect sizes easier for the reader.

[9]The following is an example of how these effect sizes are calculated: The mean implementation index for Kentucky was 4.63; thus, the z-score for Kentucky is (4.63–4.32)/0.52 = 0.60.

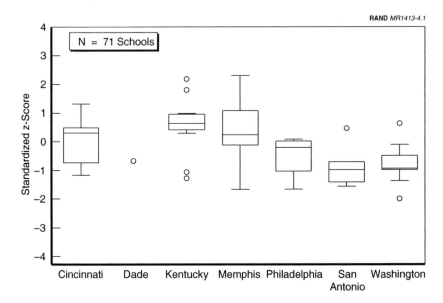

RAND *MR1413-4.1*

NOTE: Sample sizes are Cincinnati (n = 10), Dade (n = 1), Kentucky (n = 13), Memphis (n = 24), Philadelphia (n = 6), San Antonio (n = 7), Washington (n = 10).

Figure 4.1—Core Implementation Index (standardized z-scores) by Jurisdiction, Spring 1999

whiskers in the figure. Kentucky had a number of outliers, both high and low. Cincinnati also showed a great deal of spread, with schools having means that ranged from well below one standard deviation below the overall mean to well above one standard deviation above the overall mean. The differences between the highest and lowest jurisdictions were all statistically significant.

Differences in Implementation by Design Team, 1999

Comparisons among design teams reveal that CON, RW, and NARE ranked comparatively high on the core implementation index while MRSH generally ranked the lowest, reflecting the ranking we found in 1998 (Figure 4.2). CON schools had a mean that was almost one

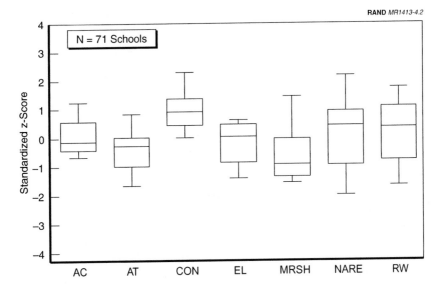

Figure 4.2—Core Implementation Index, (standardized z-scores) by Design Team, Spring 1999

standard deviation higher than the overall mean while RW and NARE schools had means that were 2/10ths and 1/10th of a standard deviation higher than the overall mean. MRSH schools had the lowest mean, over half a standard deviation below the overall mean. However, none of these differences in means was statistically significant.

The results for the core implementation index by jurisdictions and design teams are consistent with the results that we found when examining a wider set of indicators separately (see Berends, Kirby, et al. 2001, Appendix B). In addition, we also performed sensitivity analyses of our results by constructing more diverse and more inclusive indices of implementation (see Berends, 2000, for an example of a larger index). The results were consistent across these different indices.

RESULTS: CHANGES OVER TIME IN LEVELS OF IMPLEMENTATION

We measured change over time in several different ways:

- Changes in the overall mean implementation index across all schools;

- Changes in the mean implementation index by jurisdiction and design teams; and

- Changes in the overall mean implementation levels by number of years schools had been implementing in 1997 (one year, two years, three or more years) and changes in the components of the implementation index.

In order to make it easier for the reader to gauge the magnitude of the changes over time, we calculated standardized z-scores based on the mean and standard deviation of the 1997 core implementation index. This allows us to represent changes using a common metric. The mean implementation index was 4.14 in 1997 with a standard deviation of 0.61. Thus, the standardized mean for 1997 is zero, with a standard deviation of one.

Changes in Mean Level of Implementation, 1997–1999

Figure 4.3 shows the distribution of the core implementation index for all 71 schools in the longitudinal sample across the three years of data, using a standardized z-score based on the mean and standard deviation of the 1997 core implementation index. The mean implementation index rose modestly by about 0.25 of a standard deviation in 1998, and by 0.29 of a standard deviation in 1999. The difference between 1997 and 1999 was statistically significant, using a paired t-test for means.[10]

The spread declined over time as well, as can be seen from the figure. Although not shown here, the variance in mean implementation

---

[10]These are calculated as follows: The mean implementation index was 4.29 in 1998; thus the z-score for the 1998 mean is $(4.29–4.14)/0.61 \approx 0.25$. Similarly, the z-score for the 1999 mean is $(4.32–4.14)/0.61 \approx 0.29$.

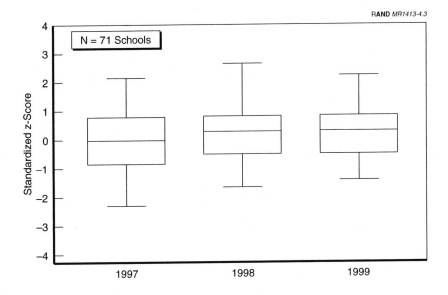

Figure 4.3—Standardized z-Scores of the Overall Implementation Index
(based on 1997 mean and standard deviation), 1997–1999

among schools declined over time. The standard deviation declined
from 0.61 in 1997 to 0.57 in 1998 and 0.52 in 1999. This decline was
not statistically significant. However, the within-school variance increased from 0.86 to 0.97 over the same time period, suggesting that
implementation did not become more "schoolwide" within a school.

Changes in Implementation Across Jurisdictions and Design

Table 4.1 shows the mean implementation level and change in the
mean over time for the jurisdictions and design teams in our sample.
Among jurisdictions, the largest gains were posted by Philadelphia
and Washington schools; these schools had among the lowest levels
of implementation in 1997. Memphis schools gained about 3/10ths
of a standard deviation and Kentucky about 2/10ths of a standard
deviation, relative to their 1997 means.

Table 4.1

Core Implementation Index: 1997 Mean and Changes over Time
(in standard deviation units), by Jurisdiction
and Design Team, 1997–1999

	Number	1997 Mean	1997 Standard Deviation	Change Between 1997 and 1999 (standard deviation units)[a]
Jurisdiction				
Cincinnati	10	4.31	0.59	0.15
Dade	1	3.14	—	—
Kentucky	13	4.56	0.34	0.19
Memphis	24	4.56	0.52	0.31
Philadelphia	6	3.47	0.33	1.80
San Antonio	7	3.79	0.79	0.10
Washington	10	3.69	0.40	0.57
Design team				
AC	4	3.62	0.39	1.87
AT	13	3.71	0.36	1.13
CON	6	4.62	0.47	0.44
EL	10	4.27	0.61	−0.09
MRSH	7	3.59	0.52	0.86
NARE	19	4.28	0.57	0.16
RW	12	4.52	0.54	−0.17
Overall mean	71	4.14	0.61	0.29

[a]The standardized change shown for each group was calculated using its own mean and standard deviation.

Among design teams, AC, AT, and MRSH showed the largest gains; schools implementing these designs had much lower than average levels of implementation in 1997. CON schools that ranked the highest in implementation in 1997 gained close to half a standard deviation, while RW and EL both posted declines of between 1/10th and 2/10ths of a standard deviation relative to their 1997 means. While it is interesting to examine changes over time by design team, one needs to be cautious in drawing inferences from these data. The small sample sizes and differences in the composition of the groups with respect to the number of years schools have been implementing designs make these comparisons less precise than one would wish.

Changes in Implementation by Years of Implementation

In order to see whether implementation has deepened over time, it is important to disaggregate the change in the mean level of implementation by number of years that schools have been implementing.

Table 4.2 shows the means for the core implementation index and its components, for schools grouped by years of implementation in 1997—one year, two years, and three or more years. Note that we do not use a standardized metric here because each group of schools has a different mean and a different standard deviation for the base year (1997). As a result, we focus on actual changes in this table. Table C.1 (Appendix C) provides the standard deviations of the core implementation index and its components. In the discussion, we provide an indication of effect sizes, where appropriate.

Note, for the first group of schools, the change between 1997 and 1998 measures the change in reported implementation levels between year 1 and year 2 of implementation, and the change between 1998 and 1999 measures the change in reported implementation levels between year 2 and year 3. For the second group of schools, the change between 1997 and 1998 measures the change in reported implementation between year 2 and year 3 of implementation and the change between 1998 and 1999, the change in reported implementation between year 3 and year 4. Similarly, for the third set of schools, the change between 1997 and 1998 measures the change in reported implementation between year 3 and year 4, while the change between 1998 and 1999 measures the change in reported implementation between year 4 and year 5 of implementation.

Changes in the Mean Implementation Level. Implementation appears to increase and deepen over the first four years after schools adopt designs, although at a decreasing rate, lending support to our hypothesis that implementation is likely to be a polynomial function of time. For example, the core implementation index:

Table 4.2

Means of the Core Implementation Index and Its Components, by Number of Years of Implementation, 1997–1999

Components of the Core Implementation Index	Schools that had been implementing for one year in 1997 (n = 31)				Schools that had been implementing for two years in 1997 (n = 22)				Schools that had been implementing for three or more years in 1997 (n = 18)			
	Mean 1997	Mean 1998	Mean 1999	Change, 1997–1999	Mean 1997	Mean 1998	Mean 1999	Change, 1997–1999	Mean 1997	Mean 1998	Mean 1999	Change, 1997–1999
Parents and community members are involved in the educational program	3.50	3.60	3.75	0.25	3.91	3.93	4.01	0.10	4.16	4.15	4.01	−0.15
Student assessments are explicitly linked to academic standards	4.07	4.47	4.71	0.64	4.62	4.73	4.87	0.25	4.78	4.81	4.82	0.04
Teachers develop and monitor student progress with personalized, individualized learning programs	3.76	3.97	4.11	0.35	4.23	4.35	4.41	0.18	4.17	4.18	4.08	−0.09
Student grouping is fluid, multiage, or multiyear	3.03	3.34	3.43	0.40	3.94	4.14	4.16	0.22	4.14	4.11	4.01	−0.13
Teachers are continual learners and team members through professional development, common planning, and collaboration	4.61	4.76	4.83	0.22	4.92	4.95	5.03	0.11	4.94	4.95	4.78	−0.16
Performance expectations are made explicit to students so that they can track their progress over time	3.91	4.27	4.29	0.38	4.45	4.50	4.63	0.18	4.49	4.51	4.44	−0.05
Core implementation index	3.80	4.12	4.17	0.37	4.34	4.43	4.52	0.18	4.43	4.44	4.33	−0.10

- Increased by 0.32 between year 1 and year 2 of implementation for those schools that reported only one year of implementation in 1997, a large change amounting to a little over half of a standard deviation;

- Increased by 0.05–0.09 between year 2 and year 3 of implementation (two groups of schools). This amounts to between 1/10th and 2/10ths of a standard deviation;

- Increased by 0.01–0.09 between year 3 and year 4 of implementation (two groups of schools) (between 0.02 and 0.18 of a standard deviation);

- Declined by –0.11 between year 4 and year 5 of implementation (almost 2/10ths of a standard deviation). Almost all these schools were NARE and RW schools.

If we further disaggregate schools in the fifth year of implementation, we find that there were five schools that had more than five years of implementation (two schools reported six years, two reported seven, and one reported ten years of implementation). While these sample sizes are small, we should note that these schools did display higher levels of implementation than those in the fifth year. For example, mean implementation levels were 4.19 for the 13 schools in the fifth year, 4.86 for the two schools in the sixth year, 4.60 for the two schools in the seventh year, and 4.68 for the one school in the tenth year of implementation. Note that the decline in implementation between the fourth and fifth years is very large: almost half a standard deviation.

Figure 4.4 summarizes the actual relationship between years of implementation and the level of implementation for schools in our sample.[11] We see a sharp increase between the first and second

---

[11] In calculating the mean level of implementation for each group, we had more than one data point for some groups, based on the three years of data. For example, schools that had been implementing for one year in 1997 had been implementing for two years in 1998. We also had some schools that had been implementing for two years in 1997. In such cases, we used a weighted average of the mean level of implementation reported by these two groups of schools, where the weights were the number of schools in each group.

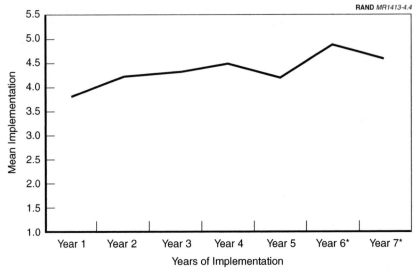

*Small sample size (two schools).

**Figure 4.4—Mean Implementation by Years of Implementation,
Longitudinal Sample**

year, modest increases from second through fourth years, and a
sharp decrease in the fifth year. Schools with more than five years
show higher levels of implementation, although the sample sizes are
quite small.

Changes in the Components of the Core Implementation Index

Looking at the other indicators, we find:

- For schools in the first four years of implementation, every indicator that comprised the core implementation index increased
  between 1997 and 1999 (Table 4.2). Some showed particularly
  large changes. For example, the indicator "student assessments
  are explicitly linked to academic standards" showed an increase
  of 0.64 for schools in the first group and 0.25 for schools in the
  second group. This was the only indicator that did not show a

decline for schools beyond the fourth year of implementation. This is likely linked to standards-based reform being adopted in most states (see Berends, Kirby, et al., in review) and the new Title I requirements under which student assessments need to be explicitly linked to content and performance standards.

- As expected, the mean for every implementation indicator is higher in every case for schools that had been implementing for two or more years compared with schools implementing for one year. This suggests that implementation does deepen with maturity. However, for schools implementing for three or more years in 1997, the changes in indicators between 1997 and 1998 are quite small and negative in some instances, and negative in almost all instances between 1998 and 1999, suggesting that implementation of these components appears to have reached a plateau in these schools, and has started to decline. This deserves further attention to understand the reasons for the decline.

Changes in Between-School Variance of Implementation

The table in Appendix C (Table C.1) shows the standard deviations for the core implementation index and its components, for schools grouped by years of implementation in 1997—one year, two years, three or more years. We summarize some findings here. The overall pattern is not very clear:

- Overall, as we had seen earlier in Figure 4.3, the variance in reported levels of mean implementation across all schools declined over time by about 15 percent.

- The variance between schools in the group that had been implementing for one year in 1997 (i.e., those relatively early in the implementation process) declined markedly between 1997 and 1999 (by about 15 percent).

- However, variance between schools remained fairly stable for the other groups.

- The indicators with the greatest between-school variability are the ones related to student grouping and to parent/community involvement. Variance with respect to the latter increased markedly over time, especially among schools that had been implementing for two or more years in 1997.

SUMMARY

The following are the main results from the updated analyses of implementation reported in this chapter.

- **Overall mean implementation across all schools increased modestly by about 3/10ths of a standard deviation.** Between-school variance declined somewhat between 1997 and 1999, but within-school variance increased.

- **There were large differences in implementation by jurisdiction.** Similar to what we found in our earlier study (Berends, Kirby, et al., 2001), Kentucky and Memphis ranked relatively high on this index, while Washington and San Antonio ranked the lowest.

- **There were differences in implementation by design in 1999.** Comparisons among design teams reveal that CON, RW, and NARE ranked comparatively high on the core implementation index while MRSH generally ranked the lowest, reflecting what we found in 1998.

- **Implementation appears to increase and deepen over the first four years after schools adopt designs, although at a decreasing rate.** Between the fourth and fifth year, however, we see a significant downturn in implementation, although a few schools showed increases beyond that time period.

Chapter Five

FACTORS AFFECTING IMPLEMENTATION

The conceptual framework outlined in Chapter Two pointed to the possible interrelationships between teacher background characteristics, school characteristics, district support, and assistance provided by design teams and implementation of the key components of designs. The previous chapter described a summary measure of implementation; however, as we noted, there is a great deal of variability in the overall indices across jurisdictions and design teams, as well as within schools. The multivariate analyses presented in this chapter allow us to analyze this variation further by partitioning it into within- and between-school components and relating this variation to a variety of teacher, school, and design team factors.[1]

VARIATION IN IMPLEMENTATION: MULTILEVEL ANALYSIS

Because the data are nested—that is, teachers are nested within schools—we use multilevel modeling techniques to provide more accurate estimates of the relationships between the dependent and independent measures (see Bryk and Raudenbush, 1992; Bryk, Raudenbush, and Congdon, 1996; Singer, 1998).

---

[1]Recall that our overall core index is comprised of the following: parents and community members are involved in the educational program; student assessments are explicitly linked to academic standards; teachers develop and monitor student progress with personalized, individualized learning programs; student grouping is fluid, multiage, or multiyear; teachers are continual learners and team members through professional development, common planning, and collaboration; and performance expectations are made explicit to students so that they can track their progress over time.

First, we partition the variance in the dependent variables into their within-school and between-school components. This provides information about whether most of the variance in the dependent variable lies between schools or within schools. Next, we estimate a set of regression coefficients in each school (Level 1), and then the constant term in the first equation (Level 1) becomes an outcome to be explained by school demographic and implementation factors (Level 2).

Specifically, for the implementation index, we estimate the following models:

Individual Teacher Model (Level 1)

$$Y_{ij} = \beta_{0j} + \beta_1 X_{ij} + r_{ij}$$

where

- Y_{ij} is the dependent variable, the teacher-reported implementation index;

- β_{0j} is the constant term, and it is the average value of the dependent variable in the school j;

- β_i is a vector of the Level 1 coefficients to be estimated with school j for the listed independent variables;

- X_{ij} is a vector of independent variables measured at the teacher level; and

- r_{ij} is the Level 1 random effect, assumed to be normally distributed with a mean of zero and constant variance.

School Context Model (Level 2)

$$\beta_{0j} = \gamma_0 + \gamma_j Z_j + u$$

where

- β_{0j} in this model is from the teacher level equation above;

- γ_0 is the constant term;
- γ_j is a vector of the Level 2 coefficients for the independent school-level variables;
- Z_j is a vector of the independent variables measured at the school level; and
- u is a Level 2 random effect.

The multilevel models described above are simple "fixed coefficient" models (Kreft and DeLeeuw, 1998). In other words, the coefficients estimating the Level 1 relationships between teacher characteristics and implementation are held constant across schools. There are no cross-level interactions between teacher and school characteristics. Thus, between-school differences are limited to differences in intercepts. In other words, the intercept for each school is the sum of the overall intercept and the sums of the school aggregate variables weighted by the school-level regression coefficients, plus error. The implementation index of each teacher is then the sum of that teacher's school intercept and the sum of the teacher-level background variables weighted by the teacher-level regression coefficients, plus error (Koretz, McCaffrey, and Sullivan, 2001).

Caveat

It is important to remember that our sample of NAS schools is not a random sample, but a sample of all those schools in the seven partnering jurisdictions that reported implementation during 1997–1999 and had survey information from teachers and principals. Despite this not being a random sample, we use multilevel modeling techniques to explore the relationships among variables at one point in time—spring 1999. These provide a more accurate description of the relationships in these NAS schools for this particular point in time. We estimate the model using the longitudinal sample and examine whether factors affecting implementation changed over time, from 1998 to 1999. We then estimate the model on the combined sample and formally test for differences between the longitudinal and the combined samples.

OPERATIONALIZING THE VARIABLES AFFECTING IMPLEMENTATION

The factors listed below are drawn from our conceptual framework. We describe the operationalization of each variable before showing its relationship with implementation in a multivariate framework.

Teacher Characteristics

Dummy variables for race-ethnicity (African American, Latino, other, vs. non-Hispanic white), educational degree (master's vs. bachelor's), total teaching experience (measured in years), and age (30 years or older vs. less than 30).

In addition, we also include three measures of teacher perceptions of their students' ability and readiness to learn (that to some degree measure teacher efficacy) and a variable that measures teacher perceptions of principal leadership:

- *Lack of basic skills is a hindrance to your students' academic success:* Teachers ranked this on a scale of 1–4 with 1 = great hindrance and 4 = not at all.

- *Lack of student discipline and inadequate parent support for students is a hindrance to your students' academic success:* These two separate survey items were summed to create one index. Each was ranked on a scale of 1–4 with 1 = great hindrance and 4 = not at all. We combined the two and obtained an average value.

- *Most of my students can learn with the school resources available to them:* This was measured on a four-point scale with 1 = strongly disagree and 4 = strongly agree.

- *Principal leadership:* Teachers were asked several questions regarding the degree of support and leadership provided by the principal. These included communicating clearly what is expected of teachers, supportive and encouraging behavior, getting resources for the school, enforcing rules for student conduct, talking with teachers regarding instructional practices, having confidence in the expertise of the teachers, and taking a personal interest in the professional development of teachers. We combined these into a summative index of principal leadership; the alpha reliability for this index was 0.87, and the correlations ranged from 0.28 to 0.65. Unfortunately, these data were not available for Dade schools because we had to administer an attenuated survey in these schools.

School Characteristics

- *Large school:* This is a dummy variable equal to one if the school is large (i.e., 400 students or more), and equal to zero otherwise.

- *Secondary school:* This is a dummy variable equal to one if the school is secondary, and equal to zero otherwise.

- *Percent student mobility:* This is a continuous variable measuring the overall student mobility reported by the principal.

- *School poverty:* This is a continuous variable measuring the percentage of students receiving free/reduced price lunch.

- *School minority composition:* This is a continuous variable measuring the percentage of students who are non-white.

- *Interaction between poverty and minority composition:* This is a continuous variable measuring the interaction between the two variables.

- *Principal leadership:* We created a school-level mean based on the sample of teachers in each school that measured principal leadership at the school level.

- *Implementation index 1997:* Because we are focusing on change and have repeated measures of implementation, we introduce the school implementation level in 1997 as a control variable. While this is not an "explanatory" variable, it makes use of the longitudinal nature of the data and allows us to see how progress in implementation is related to prior levels of implementation.

Designs and Design Team Assistance

Teacher Level

- *Communication by designs to schools:* measures the degree to which individual teachers report that the design team clearly communicated the design so that it could be well implemented. Scores for this variable range from 1 = did not communicate clearly at all to 6 = definitely communicated clearly.

- *Teacher support:* measures the extent to which teachers reported supporting or opposing the design in their school. This variable was measured on a 5-point scale, where 1 = strongly oppose and 5 = strongly support.

School Level[2]

- *Years implementing:* is number of years the school has been implementing the design with a range from two to four or more (from principal interview).

- *Communication by designs to schools:* is a school-level mean created from individual teacher reports regarding level of communication by design teams.

- *Teacher support:* is a school-level mean created from individual teacher reports; this captures the aggregated level of support in a school.

- *Set of dummy variables for designs:* Because there may be unmeasured characteristics of designs that may influence implementation in addition to those mentioned above, we also included in some models a set of dummy variables that were equal to one if the school had adopted that particular design, zero oth-

_____

[2]In analyses of earlier data, we had included a dummy variable equal to one if 60 percent or more of teachers actually voted to implement the design, zero otherwise. The models reported here did not include this variable for two reasons. First, it measured support three years ago when the schools were considering the design and we had more direct measures of support. Second, given turnover, this variable may not correctly reflect level of support in the spring of 1999.

erwise (RW is the reference category because of its relatively high levels of implementation discussed earlier).

In addition to these variables, we also created an index that measured the availability of resources at the school level to implement the designs.[3] This variable was correlated with principal leadership and was statistically insignificant when both variables were included in the model. In the interest of parsimony, it was omitted from the final model.

District Support

The models include one of the two measures of district support:

*   *Index of district support:* We ranked jurisdictions along a variety of key dimensions based on Bodilly's earlier work (1998) as well as additional interviews with districts in 1998. As we mentioned earlier, Bodilly identified several district and institutional factors that contributed to implementation: leadership backing and stability; centrality of effort; lack of crises; history of trust and cooperation; resource support; school autonomy; union support; and aligned assessment. Jurisdictions were ranked on these dimensions; the various rankings were then summed into an overall summative index of district support. The alpha reliability

---

[3]*Resources Index* was a school measure based on aggregated teacher reports about whether the school had sufficient resources to implement the designs. Teachers could respond to several questions using a 5-point scale ranging from "no resources are available" to "all are available." The resources index is a combination of a number of questions that asked the extent to which the teacher's school had the resources needed to implement the major elements of the design. These questions included:

*   Materials to describe the program;
*   Materials to support instruction;
*   Professional development for teachers;
*   Time for planning, collaboration, and development;
*   Staff or consultant to mentor, advise, and provide ongoing support;
*   Technology; and
*   Funds and funding flexibility.

The alpha reliability of this scale was 0.92 (correlations among these items ranged from 0.50 to .090).

of this index was 0.85, and the correlations ranged from 0.16 to 0.77.

- *Set of dummy variables for each jurisdiction:* Because the above index is open to criticism both on the grounds of being largely judgmental as well as being dated (based on data collected during the 1996–1997 school year), we also used the set of separate dummy variables for each jurisdiction, which was used in the earlier chapter, to test in the multilevel analyses (Memphis is the reference category). Another reason for using this set of dummy indicators rather than the index is to capture dimensions of district support that have perhaps not been captured or only partially captured by the district index.

THE ANALYSIS SAMPLE

Table 5.1 provides the means and standard deviations (SDs) for the variables in the models. The implementation index which had a mean of around 4.3 on a 1–6 scale was standardized to a mean of zero and SD = 1 in the estimated models. The analysis sample consists of about 1,200 teachers and 70 schools.[4]

Teacher Characteristics

About 63 percent of the teachers were non-Hispanic white, a little over one-fifth were African American, and about 3 percent were Hispanic. Less than 2 percent of the sample reported their race/ethnicity as "other," and about 12 percent were missing data on race/ethnicity. These latter two categories were combined into an "other/missing" category. The remaining 60–62 percent were non-Hispanic white. About half the sample had a master's degree or higher and over two-thirds were 30 years or older (a good proportion were 40 or older). They had been teaching about 16 years on average.

A large proportion of the sample felt that lack of basic skills was a hindrance to their students' academic success. This was reflected in

---

[4]Note that the sample of schools is 70, not 71. We dropped the one school in Dade for reasons explained later in this section.

Table 5.1

Descriptive Statistics of Variables in Multilevel Analysis

Variables	Mean	SD
Dependent variable		
Implementation index (range 1–6)	4.30	1.08
Implementation index (standardized)	0.00	1.00
Independent variables for teachers (n = 1092)[a]		
Race-ethnicity		
African American	0.20	
Hispanic/Latino	0.03	
Other/Missing	0.14	
Educational degree: master's or above	0.54	
Age: ≥ 30 years	0.69	
Years of teaching experience	16.57	11.45
Lack of basic skills a hindrance (range 1–4, 1 = great hindrance, 4 = not at all)	1.85	0.88
Student discipline and inadequate parent support a hindrance (range 2–8, 2 = great hindrance, 8 = not at all)	4.70	1.80
Students can learn with available resources (range 1–4, 1 = strongly disagree, 4 = strongly agree)	3.27	0.80
Principal leadership index (range 1–4, 1 = low, 4 = high)	3.23	0.65
Design-related variables		
Communication by designs to schools (range 1–6, 1 = not at all, 6 = yes, definitely)	3.88	1.67
Support for design (range 1–5, 1 = strongly oppose, 5 = strongly support)	3.59	1.23
Independent variables for schools (n = 70)[b]		
Percent poverty in 1998	66.29	29.39
Percent minority in 1997	61.52	37.42
Poverty x minority	48.99	38.57
Implementation index 1997	4.15	0.61
Years implementing	3.97	1.24
Principal leadership index (range 1–4, 1 = low, 4 = high)	3.21	0.39
Design-related variables		
Communication by designs to schools (range 1–6, 1 = not at all, 6 = yes, definitely)	3.90	1.08
Support for design (range 1–5, 1 = strongly opposed, 5 = strongly support)	3.65	0.59
Jurisdictions:		
Cincinnati	0.14	
Kentucky	0.19	
Philadelphia	0.09	
San Antonio	0.10	
Washington	0.14	
Index of district support in 1997 (range 9–24, 9 = not supportive, 24 = very supportive)	17.63	2.53
Design teams:		
AC	0.043	
AT	0.186	
CON	0.086	
EL	0.143	
MRSH	0.100	
NARE	0.271	
RW	0.171	

[a]Standard deviations are calculated from the teacher sample.

[b]Standard deviations are calculated from the school sample.

the very low mean of around 1.8 for the sample. In terms of lack of student discipline and inadequate parent support, the teachers appeared to be at the midpoint on this measure with a mean of 4.6–4.7 on a scale that ranged from 2 to 8. Teachers were surprisingly positive about their students' ability to learn, given the available resources. The mean was quite high (approximately 3.3) on a scale of 1–4.

When considering whether design teams clearly communicated the design to school staff so that it could be well implemented, we found that the average score for this teacher-level measure was about 3.9–4.0, which was somewhat higher than the mid-range on a 6-point scale ranging from not at all clear (1) to definitely clear (6). There was a great deal of variation around this mean as indicated by the standard deviation of over 1.6. In terms of support for the design, teachers again were in the middle with a mean of 3.6–3.7 (SD = 1.2).

In 1998, about 70 percent of teachers had attended a design team workshop in the past twelve months; not surprisingly, this was much lower in 1999.

School Characteristics

Poverty rate was measured as of 1998 and minority composition as of 1997. The mean poverty rate for the sample was 66 percent and the standard deviation was quite large, 29 percent. The schools also had high proportions of minority students: the mean for the sample was a little over 60 percent, with a standard deviation of 37 percent.

Given the constraints of our sample size (70 schools), we estimated several versions of the model with combinations of school characteristics. School size, school level, and student mobility were consistently insignificant in these models with small estimated effects. As a result, in the interests of parsimony and statistical power, we excluded these from the models shown here.

On average, schools were in their fourth year of implementation by 1999.

The mean school-level implementation index for 1997 was 4.15 with a standard deviation of 0.61. Note that the variability of this school-level index is much smaller than the teacher-level implementation index, the dependent variable in the model, because of aggregation at the school level.

The mean for the principal leadership index was relatively high: 3.2–3.3 on a scale of 1–4 and the standard deviation was 0.4. The schools ranged from 1.9 to 3.8 on this index. Recall that we do not have data on this variable for Dade schools. Given the importance of this variable (as shown in our earlier report, Berends, Kirby, et al., 2001), and given that we only had one school in Dade, we decided to drop this school from our multivariate analyses.

The school-level mean for communication by the design team was 3.90 on a scale of 1–6, with a large standard deviation of 1.08. The school-level mean for teacher support was 3.65 on a scale of 1–5.

The set of dummy indicators for jurisdictions shows the proportion of schools in our sample that were in particular jurisdictions. For example, 14 percent of our schools were in Cincinnati while 19 percent were in Kentucky. The largest numbers of schools in our sample were in Cincinnati, Kentucky, and Washington.

The index of district support was about 18 on a scale of 9–24.

The set of dummy variables for the design teams shows that AC schools were somewhat less well-represented in our sample, accounting for less than 4 percent of the sample. CON and MRSH schools comprised between 9 and 10 percent of the sample. The largest group was NARE schools, which constituted 27 percent of the sample, while other designs—AT, EL, RW—each accounted for between 14 and 19 percent of the sample.

MULTIVARIATE RESULTS[5]

In order to facilitate interpretation of the intercept term in the models, we centered all variables that were unique to Level 1 or Level 2 at their grand means. Centering is particularly important for the Level 1 variables both for interpretation of the intercept as well as to ensure

---

[5]We are grateful to our reviewer, Robert Croninger, for several helpful suggestions regarding the multilevel models presented here. This section benefited greatly from his constructive advice.

numerical stability (Bryk and Raudenbush, 1992: 25). Without centering, one would interpret the intercept as the expected outcome for a teacher in school j who has a value of zero on all the Level 1 predictor variables, which often does not have meaning. With centering, one can interpret the intercept as the expected outcome for a teacher in school j who is at the mean of all the predictor variables. Dummy variables were also grand-mean centered; thus the intercept term is the adjusted mean outcome in school j, adjusted for differences among units in the percentages of teachers with various characteristics. Centering the Level 2 variables simply adds to the convenience, so that the intercept term can be interpreted as the expected outcome for a school that is at the mean of the sample in terms of school characteristics.

The variables that were included at both levels (communication by the design team; teacher support; and principal's leadership) were group-mean centered at the teacher level (by subtracting the school mean score from each individual teacher's score) and the school means were then entered at Level 2 into the model. As Bryk and Raudenbush (1992) point out, this procedure avoids the assumption that the effects of variations in school means equals the effects of deviations within schools and makes the model's coefficient straightforward estimates of the within- and between-school effects.[6]

Variance Components of the Dependent Variable

Before examining the relationship between implementation and teacher and school characteristics, we begin by partitioning the variance in the dependent measure into its between- and within-school components, and examining the reliability of each school's sample mean as an estimate of its true population mean.

---

[6]Cohen, Baldi, and Rathbun (1998) point out the importance of reintroducing the school means when the Level 1 variables are group-mean centered: "A model in which the (Level 1) variables are centered around their school means sheds an important piece of information: the school mean of the variable. When the analyst fails to re-introduce this source of systematic variation appropriately elsewhere in the model, he or she posits that the actual value of the centered variable does not influence the outcome, only the relative value (that is, relative to the school mean)" (1998: 18–19).

In 1999, we find that most of the variation in the dependent variable is at the teacher level, although a substantial proportion is between schools. For example, the estimated intraclass correlation, $\hat{\rho}$, that measures the proportion of the variance in the dependent variable between schools, is 0.18. Thus between-school variance accounts for 18 percent of the total variance in the dependent variable; the within-school variance accounts for the remaining 82 percent. The between-school variance component has declined from 1998, when it accounted for 27 percent of total variance, with a corresponding increase in the within-school variance.

Such findings are not uncommon in analyses of school contextual effects on student and teacher outcomes (see Lee and Bryk, 1989; Gamoran, 1992; Berends, Kirby, et al., 2001). However, because of such differences within schools, educators, design teams, and policymakers may need to think carefully about how to implement changes throughout the school.

We can also derive an estimate of the reliability of the sample mean in any school j, $\hat{\lambda}_j$, by substituting the estimated variance components into the following equation (Bryk and Raudenbush, 1992: 63):

$$\hat{\lambda}_j = \text{Reliability (School Mean}_j) =$$

$$\{\text{Estimated Between-School Variance}/[\text{Estimated Between-School Variance} + (\text{Estimated Within-School Variance}/\text{Sample Size}_j)]\}$$

The reliability of the sample mean as an estimate of the true school mean varies from school to school, depending on sample size. However, an overall measure of reliability can be obtained by averaging across the school reliabilities. For our data, $\hat{\lambda}_j = 0.74$, which, while not as high as one would prefer, indicates that the sample means tend to be fairly reliable as indicators of the true school means.

Multivariate Results

We estimated three different models to examine the relationships between the core implementation index and teacher, design team, school, and district factors:

- Model 1: includes teacher, school, and design team characteristics (excluding the design team dummy variables);
- Model 2: includes the full set of independent variables included in Model 1, plus jurisdiction dummy variables;
- Model 3: includes the full set of independent variables included in Model 1, plus design team dummy variables and an index of district support.

As mentioned earlier, in the multilevel regression models, the intercept is modeled as a random parameter, allowed to vary between schools. The teacher variables are included as fixed effects.

The results from the models are provided in Table 5.2.

Teacher-Level Effects

The strongest effect at the teacher level was teacher perceptions of principal leadership. Teachers who ranked one point higher on the principal leadership scale relative to the school mean reported implementation levels that were over half a standard deviation higher than teachers at the mean. This effect is statistically significant and consistent across all three models.

We found some interesting differences in the level of implementation reported by African American and Hispanic teachers vs. white, non-Hispanic teachers. African American teachers tended to report significantly higher levels of implementation than white teachers (about 0.20 and 0.24 of a standard deviation higher). The coefficient for Hispanic teachers is statistically significant only in Model 2, which controls for the jurisdiction dummy variables.

Among design-related variables, both clear communication and teacher support for the design were statistically significant. Teachers who were one point higher than the school mean on both these indicators reported implementation levels that were between 0.08 and 0.12 of a standard deviation higher. These effects were consistent across the models.

The variables measuring teacher perceptions about students' readiness and ability to learn were correlated with implementation. For

Table 5.2

Multilevel Results for the Relationships of Implementation to Teacher-, School-, and Design-Related Factors

Variable	Model 1		Model 2		Model 3	
	Coefficient	Standard Error	Coefficient	Standard Error	Coefficient	Standard Error
Intercept	-2.677**	0.390	-2.424**	0.340	-2.683**	0.349
Independent variables for teachers						
Race-ethnicity						
African American	0.245**	0.067	0.210**	0.067	0.241**	0.067
Hispanic/Latino	0.098	0.147	0.319*	0.160	0.142	0.146
Other/missing	-0.039	0.082	-0.062	0.081	-0.046	0.082
Educational degree: master's or above	-0.086	0.053	-0.102*	0.051	-0.091	0.051
Age: ≥30 years	0.085	0.081	0.105	0.081	0.081	0.081
Years of teaching experience	-0.002	0.002	-0.002	0.002	-0.002	0.002
Lack of basic skills a hindrance	0.075*	0.032	0.085**	0.031	0.083**	0.031
Student discipline and inadequate parent support a hindrance	0.023	0.016	0.023	0.016	0.022	0.016
Students can learn with available resources	0.069*	0.031	0.074*	0.031	0.073*	0.031
Principal leadership	0.576**	0.049	0.572**	0.049	0.578**	0.049
Design-related variables						
Communication by designs to schools	0.122**	0.019	0.121**	0.019	0.121**	0.019
Support for design	0.077**	0.024	0.075**	0.024	0.076**	0.024

Table 5.2 (continued)

Variable	Model 1		Model 2		Model 3	
	Coefficient	Standard Error	Coefficient	Standard Error	Coefficient	Standard Error
Independent variables for schools						
Poverty × minority	-0.019**	0.005	-0.006	0.005	-0.017**	0.004
Poverty	0.012**	0.003	0.004	0.003	0.012**	0.003
Minority	0.011**	0.004	0.002	0.004	0.009**	0.003
Implementation index 1997	0.223**	0.082	0.159*	0.075	0.186*	0.081
Years implementing	0.026	0.037	-0.024	0.034	0.018	0.035
Principal leadership	0.586**	0.101	0.575**	0.090	0.555**	0.096
Design-related variables						
Communication by designs to schools	-0.005	0.046	-0.061	0.047	0.023	0.051
Support for design	0.223**	0.077	0.262**	0.068	0.215**	0.073
Jurisdiction						
Cincinnati	—a	—a	0.028	0.105	—a	—a
Kentucky	—a	—a	-0.077	0.135	—a	—a
Philadelphia	—a	—a	-0.159	0.121	—a	—a
San Antonio	—a	—a	-0.613**	0.134	—a	—a
Washington	—a	—a	-0.498**	0.178	—a	—a
Index of district support	—a	—a	—a	—a	0.001	0.015
Design teams:						
AC	—a	—a	—a	—a	0.312*	0.144
AT	—a	—a	—a	—a	0.001	0.114
CON	—a	—a	—a	—a	0.287*	0.130
EL	—a	—a	—a	—a	-0.129	0.117
MRSH	—a	—a	—a	—a	-0.223	0.127
NARE	—a	—a	—a	—a	0.089	0.155
Sample size						
Teachers	1,092		1,092		1,092	
Schools	70		70		70	

*Significant at .05 level.
**Significant at .01 level.
aExcluded from the model.

example, teachers who were one point higher than the mean with respect to their perceptions of student readiness and ability to learn were a little less than 1/10th of a standard deviation higher on the implementation index. This reinforces earlier literature on the importance of teachers' sense of efficacy in implementation (Fullan, 1991).

Mirroring what we had found earlier, teacher age, experience, and education did not appear to be important factors in implementation, controlling for everything else. This is similar to what Datnow and Castellano (2000) found in their study, although different from what Huberman (1989) reported. Teachers with a master's degree tended to report lower levels of implementation, although this is statistically significant only in Model 2.

School-Level Effects

We had chosen to enter three variables at both the teacher level and the school level, in order to be able to directly decompose the relationship between these variables and implementation into its within- and between-school components. These variables were principal leadership, communication by design team, and teacher support for the design. We discuss these first before commenting on the other school-level variables.

It is interesting that, at the school level, the effect of aggregated principal leadership is the largest predictor of between-school variance in implementation. A school that was one point higher on the school-level principal leadership scale reported implementation that was over half a standard deviation higher than a school at the mean of the index.

Teacher support was also important at the school level; schools that were one point higher than the sample mean in terms of teacher support were also likely to have implementation levels that were over 2/10ths of a standard deviation higher than schools at the mean. The effect was almost three times as large as at the teacher level.

Communication by the design team aggregated at the school level was insignificant in all three models.

An interesting question that arises in models like these is to what extent compositional or contextual effects are present. Such effects are said to occur when an aggregated school mean of a person-level characteristic has an effect on the outcome, even after controlling for the effect of the individual characteristic (Bryk and Raudenbush, 1992: 121–122). Note that in the case of principal leadership, there is no compositional effect present because the school-level effect is equal to the person-level effect. However, we do find a sizable compositional effect with respect to teacher support of approximately 0.14–0.18 of a standard deviation, even larger than the individual person effect.

As expected, the effect of prior implementation level was significant and tended to be dependent on whether jurisdiction or design team fixed effects were included in the model. Schools that ranked one point higher than average on the 1997 implementation index were likely to have implementation levels in 1999 that were about 0.15–0.22 of a standard deviation higher.

Some school demographics were significantly related to implementation, notably poverty and minority composition, both of which have positive effects on implementation in the two models not controlling for jurisdiction effects.[7] Schools that ranked 10 percentage points above the sample mean on either of these variables reported levels of implementation that were 1/10th of a standard deviation higher than schools at the sample mean. It is interesting and promising to find that schools serving largely poor or minority students report more success at whole-school reform. This may be largely a question of motivation or determination to succeed on the part of the teachers and principals in these schools. It also offers an indica-

---

[7]As mentioned earlier, we estimated several different versions of the models that included school size, school level, and student mobility. These variables were largely insignificant and were dominated by poverty and minority composition and were excluded from the final versions shown here. This is a change from our earlier results (Berends, Kirby, et al., 2001) that were based on a sample of 104 schools and 1998 data. In those models, school size, level, and student mobility did have significant effects on implementation. One plausible hypothesis for the change might be that as schools mature and gain experience with the designs, these variables become less important than variables describing the composition of the student body. Alternately, it could be that nonresponse in our panel data is leading to somewhat skewed results.

tion of the ability of some designs to help change these challenging schools.

Because poverty and minority composition are strongly correlated (the correlation coefficient is 0.76), we introduced an interaction term to see whether the combined effect of high poverty and high minority composition was different from the effects of these two variables separately. The estimated effect of the interaction term is equal to the coefficients on poverty and minority. On net, taking the combined effect of poverty and minority composition, the effect of this variable largely washes out.

There was little difference in reported implementation by number of years schools had been implementing, net of the other variables.[8]

In Model 2, controlling for other variables, we find that among the jurisdiction dummy variables, the only two statistically significant variables are those for San Antonio and Washington, both of which rank significantly lower than Memphis, the reference category.

San Antonio schools are about 6/10ths of a standard deviation lower on the implementation scale than schools in Memphis (the omitted category), after controlling for other factors. This is not surprising. Concerned about high-stakes accountability testing, in addition to the NAS designs, the district office introduced research-based instructional programs that targeted the two most basic subjects, reading and mathematics in all schools. Thus, by 1997–1998, schools were spending a substantial portion of the day on district-mandated curricular programs, rather than on design team activities. Within this context, it is not surprising that our surveys reveal very low levels of implementation of NAS designs in San Antonio.

Washington schools ranked about half a standard deviation lower than Memphis schools on the implementation index. Washington tended to rank low on indicators of district support.

These results are somewhat different from those reported in our earlier study (Berends, Kirby, et al., 2001), in which the model with jurisdiction dummy variables was dominated by the jurisdiction ef-

---

[8]A squared term to allow for nonlinearities in the relationship between years implementing and implementation was not significant in the model.

fects. These were all fairly sizable and mostly significant, even after controlling for school and teacher characteristics. The differences in results are due to the differences in the model specification and the sample. It is plausible to suggest that over time, in jurisdictions with higher implementation (Cincinnati, Memphis, Kentucky), maturity and experience with the designs ensures that the designs become institutionalized within schools, and schools are perhaps less vulnerable to, or in need of, direct district support and leadership. On the other hand, if schools that failed to receive district support also dropped out of the panel, then the district effects might well be underestimated. Based on the two studies and the RAND case studies, it is fair to infer that district and institutional factors are extremely important in ensuring the success of comprehensive school reform, particularly in the early stages of implementing the designs. This points to the need for a careful strategy to involve districts in any federal reform efforts such as CSRD.

We had earlier mentioned that we were interested in seeing whether characteristics of designs other than those measured in our models (clear communication, teacher support, attendance at design team workshop, adequacy of resources, the latter two of which are not included in models reported here) had an independent effect on implementation. We tested explicitly for these effects in Model 3. Controlling for prior implementation levels, and other factors, we find that compared with RW, the reference category, both AC and CON schools reported implementation levels that were about 3/10ths of a standard deviation higher. AC schools have made considerable progress in implementation in the last year; they tended to be at the sample mean in earlier years, and lower than RW schools. The design team had been put on notice by NAS that they might be dropped from NAS's portfolio unless they improved. As a consequence, AC reduced the number of schools in which they were during scale-up and expended time and effort on the remaining schools. It clearly paid dividends, suggesting the importance of quality support, particularly if the design has limited capacity.

In our earlier study, design team differences were statistically insignificant, controlling for other factors. It may be that over time, unobserved differences in design teams become more important making some designs easier or harder to implement.

In Model 3, we also included a measure of district support based on a summary measure from RAND's case study analysis of these districts (Bodilly, 1998). The effect of this variable was small and statistically insignificant, although positive. One reason may be the variable is too dated—given that it was based on 1996–1997 data—to reflect current realities in terms of district environment and support.

Goodness of Fit

The models we estimated explained almost all of the between-school variance in implementation. As we had mentioned earlier, 18 percent of the variance in implementation in 1999 lies between schools; school-level measures considered here explain almost all of this between-school variance (Table 5.3). In fact, the test for the residual variance components for intercepts failed to reject the null hypothesis that the conditional component of the variance between schools was zero (Singer, 1998). Another way of examining this is to compute the residual intraclass correlation, the intraclass correlation among schools that are similar across the set of characteristics included in the models.[9] In the three models, this ranges from 2 to 5 percent.

Table 5.3

Variance in Implementation Explained by the Model

	Model 1	Model 2	Model 3
Sample			
Variance between schools (t)	0.183	0.183	0.183
Variance within schools (s^2)	0.818	0.818	0.818
Model			
Variance between schools (t)	0.030	0.009	0.011
Variance within schools (s^2)	0.563	0.564	0.565
Proportion of variance between schools explained by the model	84%	95%	94%
Proportion of variance within schools explained by the model	31%	31%	31%

[9]Recall that intraclass correlation is defined as that fraction of the sum of both variance components that occurs at the school level.

Explaining within-school variance has traditionally been much more difficult. The teacher-level factors included in the models explained about 31 percent of the within-school variance, suggesting that other measures are important for explaining the differences in implementation occurring within schools.

SUMMARY

The analyses shown here further our understanding about the progress NAS schools have made in the first several years of implementation. We find that teacher reports about implementation in their school differed much more within schools than between them.

Our models strongly underscore the importance of the following factors in implementation:

- Strong principal leadership;

- Teacher support for designs and clear communication;

- A sense of teacher efficacy in terms of positive teacher perceptions and expectations about students' ability and willingness to learn;

- Teacher and school demographic characteristics (e.g., African American teacher, schools serving large numbers of poor or minority students);

- Strong district support;

- Type of design; and

- Prior level of implementation.

Many of these factors have important policy implications for the success of the current CSRD reform effort.

Chapter Six

EVIDENCE FROM THE EXIT INTERVIEWS WITH SCHOOLS THAT DISCONTINUED RELATIONSHIPS WITH NAS DESIGNS

As mentioned in the introduction, we conducted additional exit interviews with principals who reported dropping the NAS designs out of the original sample of 155 schools in either 1998 or 1999. We asked principals about the factors that contributed to the decision to drop the NAS design and what advice principals would give to schools on the verge of implementing a whole-school design. Thirty principals responded to the interviews,[1] and their responses offer some valuable lessons for the CSRD program.

Schools that dropped the design were primarily in the first or second year of implementation (about three-quarters). Six schools reported that they were in their third year of implementation and two schools in their fourth year of implementation. About 40 percent of the schools were NARE schools in Kentucky. About a quarter of the schools were Dade schools that had been implementing a variety of designs. A little under half were secondary schools. Because of the preponderance of NARE schools, the poverty and minority composition of the schools was somewhat below the NAS average (59 percent

---

[1]As we mentioned earlier, it is difficult to calculate an attrition rate (i.e., schools that dropped the design as a percentage of the total sample) for the sample as a whole. Some schools that did not respond may well have dropped the design. Out of the 184 schools at the beginning of scale-up and excluding the 12 Pittsburgh schools that were later dropped from the study, at least 41 schools out of 172 had dropped the design, giving us a lower-bound attrition rate of approximately 24 percent.

and 54 percent compared with the NAS averages of 66 percent and 62 percent).

FACTORS THAT CONTRIBUTED TO THE DECISION TO DROP THE DESIGN

Table 6.1 lists the factors that schools cited as having contributed "a fair amount" or "a great deal" to the decision to drop the design. The table gives the frequency of each answer. The answers are not mutually exclusive as schools could cite several categories as being

Table 6.1

Factors Contributing to the Decision to Drop the NAS Design

Factors	Number of schools answering "fair amount" or "great deal"
Lack of funding to pay for the design	21
Lack of funding to pay for professional development	19
Lack of support from the district	12
The design was not what you and your staff expected at the time you adopted it	9
Other reasons	9[a]
Implementing the design required too much work for your staff	8
Lack of teacher support	7
Materials and/or training provided by the design team were of poor quality	6
Lack of alignment between the design and district or state mandated tests	5
Lack of alignment between the design and district- or state-mandated curriculum requirement	5
Dissatisfaction with the design team	4
Large turnover among staff	4
New principal	2
Problematic relationships among staff	0
Parental opposition to the design	0
Total Number of Schools	30

[a]These included lack of funding, lack of support from the design team, lack of support from the state, not enough direction given to teachers, and "good but boring materials from the design team."

important. Most schools ranked between one and four factors as having a great deal of influence on the decision to drop the design.

Funding to pay for the design and for professional development for teachers were the primary reasons for dropping the design, while lack of support from the district and the state ranked second. Schools were also unhappy about the amount of effort required on the part of teachers to implement the designs, and the materials or training provided by the design teams. Nine principals cited "other reasons" but on a closer reading, these reasons appeared to relate in some way to lack of funding, lack of support at the state level, and dissatisfaction with the assistance provided by the design teams.

Eleven schools reported that they were planning to replace the design with some other reform effort. Seven schools reported that this new program was more curriculum-centered than the design, and four reported that it was another whole-school reform. Interestingly, although the schools were dropping the design, almost half reported that they planned to continue some elements or aspects of the designs.

Principals were asked what advice they would give to schools that were considering adopting whole-school designs. Some of the comments are noteworthy:

> "Make sure you know everything up front—costs, training, and ask for five year commitments. Make arrangements for time."

> "First consider what type of kids you are serving. . . . These programs do not fit every building. Make sure you have enough money for training. If you don't have the money, there's no use jumping into it."

> "Do it systematically, be careful with selection. Make sure the selections are successful in a variety of different settings and have data to prove it. Make sure you have faculty buy-in."

> "Make sure all teachers and stakeholders understand the need and design of the change. . . . After all, faculty is going to be doing it."

"Make sure you have funding and support from state and district."

"Research the design thoroughly. Visit schools that have imple-mented program. Call the state and see how long they project the program's continuation."

"Be patient in seeing significant change. With staff, people accept change differently. Change takes time and new learning."

This advice resonates with findings discussed earlier and would be well-heeded by schools involved in the whole-school restructuring initiatives.

Chapter Seven

CONCLUSIONS AND POLICY IMPLICATIONS

NAS's mission is to help schools and districts significantly raise the achievement of large numbers of students with design-based assistance. While each design is unique, each aims to restructure the entire school emphasizing changes in organization and governance, the professional lives of teachers, content and performance expectations, curriculum and instructional strategies, and parent and community involvement.

This chapter provides an overview of the conclusions of our study and some policy implications. Although we largely focus on findings from the current study, where appropriate, we refer to findings from the larger set of RAND work on NAS schools.

IMPLEMENTATION IN NAS SCHOOLS

- **Implementation increased modestly from 1997 to 1999. The between-school variance decreased somewhat over time, while the within-school variance increased.**

- **There were large differences in implementation by jurisdiction in 1999.** Similar to what we found in our earlier study (Berends, Kirby, et al., 2001), Kentucky and Memphis ranked relatively high on this index, while Washington and San Antonio ranked the lowest.

- **There were differences in implementation by design team in 1999.** Comparisons among design teams reveal that CON, RW, and NARE ranked comparatively high on the core implementation index while MRSH generally ranked the lowest, reflecting what we found in 1998.

- **Implementation appears to increase and deepen over the first four years after schools adopt designs, although at a decreasing rate.** Between the fourth and fifth years, however, we see a significant downturn in implementation, although a few schools with more years of implementation continued to show progress.

FACTORS AFFECTING IMPLEMENTATION IN NAS SCHOOLS

The process of changing entire schools to improve student learning opportunities is complex and difficult, because so many actors are involved and so many factors have to be aligned to support change. Several factors emerge from our research as fostering high-quality and coherent implementation in the types of schools in the sample, perhaps the most important of which is principal leadership.

Schools

Strong Principal Leadership. Schools that reported having strong principal leaders had implementation levels over half a standard deviation above schools at the sample average. In addition, individual teachers' beliefs about principal leadership were important in explaining within-school variance in implementation. Our findings suggest that effective and supportive principal leaders are likely to both increase and deepen implementation in a school. For example, if most or all the teachers in a school view the principal as a strong leader, this will likely lead to reduced variance within a school and help the design become more schoolwide. The importance of principal leadership for establishing effective schools has been emphasized by researchers for decades (Edmonds, 1979; Purkey and Smith, 1983; Rosenholtz, 1985), so it is not surprising that such leadership is critical for the implementation of NAS designs. While not surprising, the crucial role that principal leadership plays with respect to implementation should not be overlooked when adopting and implementing whole-school reforms.

School Composition. Taking into account other factors related to teachers, design teams, and districts, we found that poverty and minority composition of students were related to implementation, both in a positive direction. Teacher-reported implementation levels were higher in higher poverty schools and among schools with high percentages of minority students. However, the interaction of high poverty and high minority composition appeared to have a negative effect on implementation.

Our discussion has focused thus far on the net influence of each factor. However, it is important to emphasize that schools often face a multiplicity of challenges, and the interaction among these factors can set these schools back considerably in their attempts to implement school designs. Bodilly (1998) found, for example, that schools that were beset with a combination of two or more negative factors such as internal tensions, leadership turnover, forced adoptions of designs, or poor understanding of designs, ranked very low on implementation. Thus, schools need stable leadership and capacity and commitment on the part of the teachers to make the designs work.

Prior Level of Implementation. We find that schools with higher levels of prior implementation tended to make steady progress over time. Thus, it becomes important to make sure that schools have the resources, willingness, and the capacity to implement designs right from the beginning. A strong initial effort is likely to pay off in the long run in terms of higher implementation; otherwise, schools are likely to fall further behind.

Teachers

Sense of Teacher Efficacy. In our analyses, we found that teacher perceptions of students and their readiness to learn were all significantly related to teacher-reported levels of implementation. Teachers with a greater sense of efficacy (i.e., those who believed strongly that lack of basic skills was not a hindrance to their students' academic success, or that students can learn with the resources available) also reported higher implementation than those who felt otherwise.

These are conditions commonly reported by urban schools, highlighting the importance of getting teachers behind the adopted model, and providing them with supports and resources to allow them to teach to high standards.

Teacher Support for the Model. This variable was important in explaining both within-school and between-school variance in implementation. Supportive teachers implemented at a higher level within a school; the greater the degree of overall school-level support, the higher the implementation. This highlights the importance of getting teachers behind the adopted model; supportive teachers tend to reinforce and enhance implementation, not merely at the individual teacher level but at the school level as well.

Design Teams

Importance of Clear Communication. At the teacher level, not surprisingly, we find that clear communication on the part of the design aids implementation. In her case study work, Bodilly (1998) identified five elements related to design teams that were important contributors to design implementation:

- A stable team with the capacity to serve a growing number of schools;

- Ability to communicate the design well to schools;

- Effective marketing to the district and ability to gain needed resources to implementation;

- Greater relative emphasis on core elements of schooling (curriculum, instruction, student assignment, student assessment, and professional development) rather than a more systemic approach; and

- Stronger implementation support to schools with whole-school training, facilitators, extensive training days, quality checks, and materials.

Our findings and those of the earlier study (Berends, Kirby, et al., 2001) highlight the importance of clear communication to teachers and design team support in the form of resources in encouraging high levels of implementation.

Type of Design. Our study found that overall certain designs had markedly higher levels of implementation: CON, NARE, and RW, while others such as MRSH had markedly lower levels of implementation. In the multivariate model, controlling for other factors such as prior implementation and school characteristics, we do not find many differences among designs, with two exceptions: CON schools and AC schools made steady progress over this time period. AC schools, which in 1997 were at the low-end of the implementation index, have made marked progress in implementation over the two years. This may be due to unobserved characteristics of the designs themselves that make them easier or harder to implement in schools already facing several challenges in terms of poverty, lack of resources, and the capacity to implement designs—a critical issue for future research to address.

Districts

Importance of Stable Leadership, Resources, and Support. Districts play several important roles in fostering/hindering implementation, including:

- Initial matching and selection;
- Encouraging support by the design team;
- Creating a supportive environment with supportive
  - Political leadership;
  - Regulatory policies; and
  - Consistent coherent funding stream.

Bodilly (1998) identified several district and institutional factors that contributed to implementation. These were leadership backing and stability at the district level; centrality of the NAS initiative to the district's agenda; lack of crisis situations; history of trust and cooperation; availability of resources for transformation; school-level authority and/or autonomy; union support; district accountability; and assessment systems that were compatible with those of the designs.

The analyses reported here as well as in our earlier work (Berends, Kirby, et al., 2001) showed that the level of implementation varied significantly across districts. In our analysis, we found that Memphis and Kentucky ranked high on these indicators of support and ranked high in implementation; others, such as San Antonio and Washington lagged far behind on both support indicators and implementation.

Thus, it is clear that several factors need to be aligned for designs to be well-implemented in schools. Without strong principal leadership, without teachers who support the designs and have a strong sense of teacher efficacy, without district leadership and support, without clear communication and provision of materials and staff support on the part of design teams, implementation is likely to lag far behind. These are sobering and important lessons for federal, state, and local efforts aimed at comprehensive school reform.

CORE COMPONENTS OF THE DESIGNS

This appendix discusses in more detail the concepts relating to the core components of the design.

Organization and governance refer to the authority relations among the various parties in the school. An example of changing governance arrangements is reorganizing the decisionmaking processes for budgets and staffing to include teachers and other school employees and parents. Giving authority to the school site has received a great deal of attention in the education community. According to Murphy (1992) the central focus on governance restructuring stems from a belief that change must reside with those who are closest to the learners (see also Bryk et al., 1998a; Smith, Scoll, and Link, 1996). NAS and many of the designs strongly share this belief.

The professional life of teachers refers to the roles and relationships in which the teachers participate during the school day. In effect, when referring to restructuring schools, particularly those in poor, urban areas, this involves overhauling the conditions under which teachers work by changing their responsibilities and tasks and by developing a more professional culture in schools (Newmann et al., 1996; Murphy, 1992; Sykes, 1990; Wise, 1989). In contrast to teachers working in isolation without contact with their colleagues (see Louis and Miles, 1990; Lortie, 1970), design teams aim to build a collaborative environment for teachers. Thus, it is important to understand the extent to which teachers collaborate and engage in activities together such as professional development, common planning time, and critiquing each other's instruction.

Each of the designs aims to bring all students to high standards, even though each may differ in the process to attain this goal. To monitor whether designs are making progress toward this end, critical indicators might include the degree to which: (a) student assessments are explicitly linked to academic standards, (b) teachers make performance expectations explicit to students, and (c) the curriculum and performance standards are consistent and coherent across grade levels.

Most of the designs are concerned with shaping student experiences within classrooms to further their academic achievement growth. NAS designs embrace alternative instructional strategies that involve different relationships between teachers and students and between students and subject matter. Yet, again, each design differs somewhat in the specific nature of these activities. Conventional classrooms are often characterized as teachers talking *at* students and filling their heads with knowledge, with students responding with the correct answers at appropriate times (see Gamoran et al., 1995; Sizer, 1984; Powell, Farrar, and Cohen, 1985). In contrast, design teams tend to emphasize alternative instructional practices such as students working in small groups, using manipulatives, engaging in student-led discussions, or working on projects that span a long period of time (e.g., a marking period or semester).

The design teams also address a particular set of instructional strategies revolving around student grouping arrangements. How students are grouped for instruction and the effects of this on student achievement are subjects of heated debate among educators and researchers (see Slavin, 1987, 1990; Gamoran and Berends, 1987; Oakes, Gamoran, and Page, 1992; Hallinan, 1994; Oakes, 1994). Yet, most researchers agree that alternatives to inflexible grouping arrangements are worth further exploration. Thus, the NAS designs have experimented with such alternative student groupings. For example, students within an EL or CON design may have the same teacher for a couple years. RW emphasizes flexible uses of grouping by organizing students according to their achievement levels in reading for part of the day and mixing achievement levels for other subjects. These groupings are assessed every eight weeks or so to see if students would be better served by being placed in a different group. In short, each of the designs is sensitive to the issue of ability grouping and is working with schools to group students in more effective ways.

Conventional wisdom suggests that the parent-child relationship and parent involvement in the child's education are critical components of school success. The NAS designs have embraced this issue as well. Several of the designs aim to have individuals or teams within the schools serve as resources to students and families to help integrate the provision of social services to them (e.g., AT and RW). Other designs emphasize students applying their learning in ways that directly benefit the community (e.g., AC, EL, and NARE). Of course, each design desires that parents and community members be involved in positive ways in the educational program.

DEFINING THE LONGITUDINAL SAMPLE OF NAS SCHOOLS

In this section, we present the details of the longitudinal sample of NAS schools.

THE POPULATION OF NEW AMERICAN SCHOOLS FOR THE LONGITUDINAL EVALUATION

The original sample of schools consisted of those schools initiating implementation of NAS designs in eight jurisdictions that NAS named as its partners during scale-up in either 1995–1996 or 1996–1997.[1] These eight jurisdictions included:

- Cincinnati;
- Dade;
- Kentucky;
- Memphis;
- Philadelphia;
- Pittsburgh;
- San Antonio; and
- Washington state.

---

[1]At the time we decided on the longitudinal sample of schools, Maryland and San Diego were not far enough along in their implementation to warrant inclusion in RAND's planned data collection efforts. Since then, several of the design teams report that they are implementing in Maryland and San Diego.

The choice of these jurisdictions reflected RAND's desire to obtain a sample including all the designs that were participating in the scale-up phase and the judgment that the costs of working in the additional jurisdictions would not yield commensurate benefits. While jurisdictions and their support of the NAS reform will no doubt continue to change over time, these jurisdictions reflect a range of support for implementation—from relatively supportive to no support at all (see Bodilly, 1998).

THE 1998 FINAL ANALYSIS SAMPLE

Our aim was to collect data on all the NAS schools that were to be implementing within the partner jurisdictions. NAS believed that as of early fall 1996, there were 256 schools implementing NAS designs across these eight jurisdictions. However, based on conversations with design teams, jurisdictions, and the schools, the sample was reduced to 184 schools for several reasons:

- There were 51 Roots & Wings schools in Dade that were low-performing and on the verge of serious sanctions, so the district promised these schools that they would not be burdened with researchers.

- An additional 21 schools declined to participate because they did not want to be burdened with research, were not implementing, or dropped the design.

Thus, for our surveys of teachers and principals, the target sample was 184 schools (see Table B.1). To some extent, limiting our sample to schools that were implementing and were not on the verge of serious sanctions biases our sample in a positive direction in terms of expected implementation.

Of the 184 schools in our 1997 sample, we completed interviews with 155 principals. Based on our interviews with principals in the spring of 1997, most of these schools reported they were indeed implement-

Table B.1

**1997 Target Sample for RAND's Longitudinal Sample:
Principal Interviews and Teacher Surveys**

Jurisdiction	Design Team							Total
	AC	AT	CON	EL	MRSH	NARE	RW	
Cincinnati			5	5			6	16
Dade	5		4	1	3		4	17
Kentucky						51		51
Memphis	5	5	5	5	4		9	33
Philadelphia		12	4		2			18
Pittsburgh						12		12
San Antonio				8	5			13
Washington		8				16		24
Total	10	25	18	19	14	79	19	184

ing a design.[2] Yet, some were not. Figure B.1 shows that 25 of the 155 schools (about 15 percent) reported that they were in an exploratory year or a planning year with implementation expected in the future. About 85 percent (130/155) of the schools for which we had teacher, principal, and district data reported implementing a NAS design to some extent.[3]

Because our interest is in understanding the specific activities that are occurring within the 130 schools that were implementing a NAS design to some extent (the non-white areas of Figure B.1), we limited our analysis sample to these 130 schools.

In the spring of 1998, all 184 schools were once again surveyed. The completed sample size of implementing schools consisted of 142

---

[2]The first question we asked principals was about the status of the school's partnership with a NAS design. Principals could respond that they were in an exploratory year (that is, the school has not committed to a design yet); in a planning year (the school has partnered with a design team and is planning for implementation next school year); in initial implementation for part of the school (i.e., a subset of the staff is implementing); continuing implementation for part of the school; in initial implementation for the whole school (i.e., all or most of the staff are working with the design); or continuing implementation for the whole school.

[3]These were schools that had complete principal data, at least five teachers responding to the teacher surveys, and complete district data.

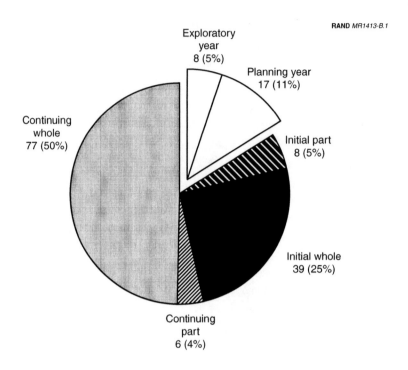

RAND *MR1413-B.1*

Figure B.1—Principal Reports of Implementation Status, Spring 1997

schools. However, the overlap between the 1997 and 1998 samples was incomplete. For purposes of this analysis, which is partly longitudinal in nature, we limited the analysis sample to schools that met two criteria:

- Schools were implementing in both 1997 and 1998; and
- Schools had complete data (i.e., from teachers and principals) in both years.

Of the 130 schools implementing in 1997 for which we had complete data, seven had either dropped the design or had reverted to planning and another 17 had missing or incomplete data. Thus, 106 schools met both criteria. Figure B.2 shows the derivation of the sample.

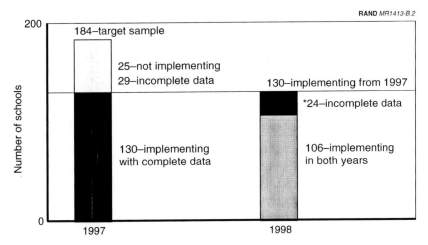

RAND *MR1413-B.2*

*6–dropped design; 1–reverted to planning; 17–missing principal or teacher data.

Figure B.2—Derivation of the Sample Analyzed in the Previous Study

Of these 106 schools, there were two schools in Pittsburgh that we later discovered were not implementing and had dropped the design. In fact, throughout RAND's monitoring of the schools in Pittsburgh, there were severe budget crises. RAND's site visits and principal phone interviews consistently revealed that NAS implementation in Pittsburgh was not taking place (also see Bodilly, 1998). As a result, these two schools (and Pittsburgh) were excluded from the analyses reported here; our final sample for the analysis consisted of 104 schools across seven jurisdictions.

TABLE OF STANDARD DEVIATIONS FOR THE CORE
IMPLEMENTATION INDEX AND ITS COMPONENTS

Table C.1
Table of Standard Deviations for the Core Implementation Index and Its Components

Components of the Core Implementation Index	Schools that had been implementing for one year in 1997 (n = 31)				Schools that had been implementing for two years in 1997 (n = 22)				Schools that had been implementing for three or more years in 1997 (n = 18)			
	SD 1997	SD 1998	SD 1999	Change, 1997–1999	SD 1997	SD 1998	SD 1999	Change, 1997–1999	SD 1997	SD 1998	SD 1999	Change, 1997–1999
Parents and community members are involved in the educational program	0.79	0.90	0.82	0.03	0.64	0.94	1.01	0.37	0.73	0.88	0.89	0.16
Student assessments are explicitly linked to academic standards	0.57	0.73	0.52	–0.05	0.63	0.49	0.71	0.08	0.66	0.61	0.66	0.00
Teachers develop and monitor student progress with personalized, individualized learning programs	0.67	0.69	0.58	–0.09	0.54	0.49	0.57	0.03	0.75	0.68	0.69	–0.06
Student grouping is fluid, multiage, or multiyear	1.16	1.34	1.13	–0.03	1.15	1.14	1.00	–0.15	1.14	1.16	1.09	–0.05
Teachers are continual learners and team members through professional development, common planning, and collaboration	0.58	0.68	0.43	–0.15	0.51	0.46	0.54	0.03	0.69	0.68	0.58	–0.11
Performance expectations are made explicit to students so that they can track their progress over time	0.66	0.52	0.51	–0.15	0.39	0.44	0.53	0.14	0.61	0.63	0.59	–0.02
Core implementation index	0.57	0.55	0.48	–0.09	0.50	0.53	0.52	0.02	0.54	0.61	0.52	–0.02

REFERENCES

American Association of School Administrators. (1995). *Great expectations: Understanding the new Title I.* Washington, DC: Author.

Bascia, N. (2000). "The impact of mandated change on teachers." In A. Hargreaves & N. Bascia (eds.), *The sharp edge of change: Teaching, leading and the realities of reform.* London: Falmer Press.

Berends, M. (1999). *Assessing the progress of New American Schools: A status report.* Santa Monica, CA: RAND (MR-1085-ED).

Berends, M. (2000). "Teacher-reported effects of New American Schools' designs: Exploring relationships to teacher background and school context." *Educational evaluation and policy analysis,* 22(1), pp. 65–82.

Berends, M., Grissmer, D. W., Kirby, S. N., & Williamson, S. (1999). "The changing American family and student achievement trends." *Review of sociology of education and socialization,* 23, pp. 67–101.

Berends, M., & King, B. (1994). "A description of restructuring in nationally nominated schools: Legacy of the iron cage?" *Educational policy* 8(1), pp. 28–50.

Berends, M., Kirby, S. N., Naftel, S., & McKelvey, C. (2001). *Implementation and performance in New American Schools: Three Years into scale-up.* Santa Monica, CA: RAND.

Berends, M., Kirby, S. N., Naftel, S., & Sloan, J. S. (in review). *The National Longitudinal Survey of Schools: Preliminary findings.* Washington, DC: U.S. Department of Education.

Berends, M., & Bodilly, S. (forthcoming). "New American Schools' scale-up phase: Lessons learned to date." In S. Stringfield, A. Datnow, and S. Yonezawam (eds.). *Scaling up designs for educational improvement.* Baltimore: Johns Hopkins University Press.

Berends, M., Chun, J., Schuyler, G., Stockly, S., & Briggs, R. J. (In Press). *Challenges of Conflicting School Reforms: Effects of New American Schools in a high-poverty district.* Santa Monica, CA: RAND (MR-1483-EDU).

Berman, P., & McLaughlin, M. (1978). *Federal programs supporting educational change,* vol. VII: *Factors affecting implementation and continuation.* Santa Monica, CA: RAND.

Bodilly, S. J. (1998). *Lessons from New American Schools' scale-up phase: Prospects for bringing designs to multiple schools.* Santa Monica, CA: RAND (MR-945-NAS).

Bodilly, S. J. (2001). *New American Schools' designs: How designs evolved and why.* Santa Monica, CA: RAND (MR-1288-NAS).

Bodilly, S. J., & Berends, M. (1999). "Necessary district support for comprehensive school reform." In G. Orfield and E. H. DeBray (eds.). *Hard work for good schools: Facts not fads in Title I reform.* Boston, MA: The Civil Rights Project, Harvard University, pp. 111–119.

Borman, K. M., Cookson, Jr., P. W., Sadovnik, A. R., & Spade, J. Z. (eds.) (1996). *Implementing educational reform: Sociological perspectives on educational policy.* Norwood, N.J.: Ablex Publishing Corporation.

Bryk, A. S., & Driscoll, M. E. (1988). "The high school as community: Contextual influence, and consequences for students and teachers." Madison, WI: National Center on Effective Secondary Schools, Wisconsin Center for Education Research, University of Wisconsin-Madison.

Bryk, A. S., & Raudenbush, S. W. (1992). *Hierarchical linear models: Applications and data analysis methods.* Newbury Park, CA: Sage Publications.

Bryk, A., Lee, V., & Holland, P. (1993). *Catholic schools and the common good.* Cambridge, MA: Harvard University.

Bryk, A. S., Raudenbush, S. W., & Cogdan, R. T. (1996). *HLM: Hierarchical linear and nonlinear modeling with the HLM/2L and HLM/3L programs.* Chicago: Scientific Software International.

Bryk, A. S., Sebring, P. B., Kerbow, D., Rollow, S., & Easton, J. Q. (1998a). *Charting Chicago school reform: Democratic localism as a lever for change.* Boulder, CO: Westview.

Bryk, A. S., Thum, Y., Eaton, M. J. Q., & Luppescu, S. (1998b). *Academic productivity of Chicago public elementary schools.* Chicago: Consortium on Chicago School Research.

Cohen, J., Baldi, S., & Rathbun, A. (1998). *Hierarchical linear models and their application in educational research.* Washington, DC: American Institutes for Research.

Coleman, J. S., Campbell, E. Q., Hobson, C. J., McPartland, J., Mood, A. M., Weinfeld, F. D., & York, R. L. (1966). *Equality of educational opportunity.* Washington, DC: U.S. Government Printing Office.

Consortium for Policy Research in Education (1998). "States and districts and comprehensive school reform." CPRE Policy Brief. Philadelphia, PA: University of Pennsylvania Graduate School of Education.

Darling-Hammond, L. (2000). "Teacher quality and student achievement: A review of state policy evidence." *Education policy analysis archives,* 8(1), pp. 1–32.

Datnow, A. (1998). *The gender politics of educational change.* London: Falmer Press.

Datnow, A. (2000a). "Gender politics and school reform." In A. Hargreaves & N. Bascia (eds.). *The sharp edge of change:*

Teaching, leading, and the realities of reform. London: Falmer Press.

Datnow, A. (2000b). Implementing an externally developed school restructuring design. *Teaching and change,* 7(2), pp. 147–171.

Datnow, A., & Castellano, J. (2000). "Teachers' responses to Success for All: How beliefs, experiences, and adaptations shape implementation." *American educational research journal,* 37(3), pp. 775–799.

Datnow, A., & Stringfield, S. (2000). "Working together for reliable school reform." *Journal of education for students placed at risk,* 5(1&2), pp. 183–204.

Datnow, A., & Stringfield, S. (1997). *School effectiveness and school improvement,* 8(1).

Day, C., Harris, A., Hadfield, M., Toley, H., & Beresford, J. (2000). *Leading schools in times of change.* Buckingham, England: Open University Press.

Desimone, L. (2000). *Making comprehensive school reform work.* New York: ERIC Clearinghouse on Urban Education, Teachers College.

Edmonds, R. R. (1979). "Effective schools for the urban poor." *Educational leadership,* 37, pp. 15–24.

Education Commission of the States. (1999). *Comprehensive school reform: Five lessons from the field.* Denver, CO: Author.

Elmore, R. (2000). *Building a new structure for school leadership.* Washington, DC: The Albert Shanker Institute.

Elmore, R. F., & Rothman, R. (eds.). (1999). *Testing, teaching, and learning: A guide for states and school districts.* Committee on Title I testing and assessment, National Research Council. Washington, DC: National Academy Press.

Fordham, S., & Ogbu, J. (1986). "Black students' school success: Coping with the burden of acting white." *Urban review,* 18(3), pp. 176–206.

Foster, M. (1993). "Resisting racism: Personal testimonies of African-American teachers." In L. Weis & M. Fine (eds.). *Beyond silenced voices: Class, race, and gender in United States schools.* Albany, NY: State University of New York Press, pp. 273–288.

Fullan, M. G. (1991). *The new meaning of educational change.* New York: Teachers College Press.

Fullan, M. (2001). *Leading in a culture of change.* San Francisco: Jossey-Bass.

Gamoran, A. (1987). "The stratification of high school learning opportunities." *Sociology of education,* 60, pp. 135–155.

Gamoran, A. (1992). "The variable effects of high school tracking." *American sociological review,* 57, pp. 812–828.

Gamoran, A., & Berends, M. (1987). "The effects of stratification in secondary schools: Synthesis of survey and ethnographic research." *Review of educational research,* 57, pp. 415–435.

Gamoran, A., & Dreeben, R. (1986). Coupling and control in educational organizations. *Administrative science quarterly,* 31, pp. 612–632.

Gamoran, A., Nystrand, M., Berends, M., & LePore, P. C. (1995). "An organizational analysis of the effects of ability grouping." *American educational research journal,* 32, pp. 687–715.

Glennan, T. K., Jr. (1998). *New American Schools after six years.* Santa Monica, CA: RAND (MR-945-NAS).

Grissmer, D. W., & Flanagan, A. (1998). *Exploring rapid achievement gains in North Carolina and Texas.* Washington, DC: National Education Goals Panel.

Hallinan, M. T. (1994). "Tracking: From theory to practice." *Sociology of education,* 67(2), pp. 79–83.

Hargreaves, A. (1994). *Changing teachers, changing times.* New York: Teachers College Press.

Hatch, T. (2000). *What happens when multiple improvement initiatives collide.* Menlo Park, CA: Carnegie Foundation for the Advancement of Teaching.

Hoffer, T. (1992). "Effects of community type on school experiences and student learning." Paper presented to the 1992 annual meeting of the American Educational Research Association, San Francisco, CA.

Huberman, M. (1989). "The professional life cycle of teachers." *Teachers College Record,* 91(2), pp. 30–57.

Jencks, C. S., Smith, M., Acland, H., Bane, M. J., Cohen, D., Gintis, H., Heyns, B., & Michelson, S. (1972). *Inequality: A reassessment of the effect of family and schooling in America.* New York: Basic Books.

Jennings, J. F. (1996). "Travels without Charley." *Phi Delta Kappan,* 78, pp. 11–16.

Jennings, J. F. (1998). *Why national standards and tests? Politics and the quest for better schools.* Thousand Oaks, CA: Sage Publications.

Keltner, B. (1998). *Resources for transforming New American Schools: First year findings.* Santa Monica, CA: RAND (IP-175).

Kirby, S. N., Berends, M., Naftel, S., & Sloan, J. S. (in review). *Comprehensive School Reform Demonstration (CSRD) schools: Early findings on implementation.* Santa Monica, CA: RAND.

Koretz, D. M. (1996). "Using student assessments for educational accountability." In E. A. Hanushek and D. W. Jorgenson (eds.). *Improving America's Schools: The role of incentives.* Washington, DC: National Academy Press, pp. 171–196.

Koretz, D. M., & Barron, S. I. (1998). *The validity of gains in scores on the Kentucky Instructional Results Information System (KIRIS).* Santa Monica, CA: RAND (MR-1014-EDU).

Koretz, D. M., McCaffrey, D., & Sullivan, T. (2001). *Using TIMSS to analyze correlates of performance variation in mathematics.*

NCES Working Paper 2001-05. Washington, DC: National Center for Education Statistics, U.S. Department of Education.

Kreft, I., & De Leeuw, J. (1998). *Introducing multilevel modeling.* Thousand Oaks, CA: Sage Publications.

Lee, V. E., & Bryk, A. S. (1989). "A multilevel model of the social distribution of high school achievement." *Sociology of education,* 62(3), pp. 172–192.

Lee, V. E., Bryk, A. S., & Smith, J. B. (1993). "The organization of effective secondary schools." *Review of research in education,* 19, pp. 171–267.

Lee, V. E., & Smith, J. B. (1995). "Effects of high school restructuring and size on early gain in achievement and engagement." *Sociology of education,* 68(4), pp. 241–270.

Lee, V. E., & Smith, J. B. (1997). "High school size: Which works best and for whom?" *Educational evaluation and policy analysis,* 19(3), pp. 205–227.

Lipppman, L., Burns, S., & McArthur, E. (1996). *Urban schools: The challenge of location and poverty.* Washington, DC: National Center for Education Statistics, U.S. Department of Education.

Lortie, D. (1970). *School teacher.* Chicago, IL: University of Chicago Press.

Louis, K. S., & Marks, H. M. (1998). "Does professional community affect the classroom? Teachers' work and student experiences in restructuring schools." *American journal of education* 106(4), pp. 532–575.

Louis, K. S., & Miles, M. B. (1990). *Improving the urban high school: What works and why.* New York: Teachers College Press.

McLaughlin, M. W. (1990). "The RAND Change Agent Study revisited: Macro perspectives and micro realities." *Educational researcher,* 19(9), pp. 11–16.

McLaughlin, M. W., & Marsh, D. D. (1978). "Staff development and school change." *Teachers college record,* 80(1), pp. 69–94.7.

McLaughlin, M., & Talbert, J. (2001). *Professional communities and the work of high school teaching.* Chicago, IL: University of Chicago Press.

McLaughlin, M., W., Talbert, J. E., & Bascia, N. (eds.) (1990). *The contexts of teaching in secondary school: Teachers' realities.* New York: Teachers College Press.

Meyer, R. H. (1996). "Value-added indicators of school performance." In E. A. Hanushek and D. W. Jorgenson (eds.). *Improving America's schools: The role of incentives.* Washington, DC: National Academy Press, pp. 197–224.

Montjoy, R., & O'Toole, L. (1979). "Toward a theory of policy implementation: An organizational perspective." *Public administration review,* September/October, pp. 465–476.

Muncy, D., & McQuillan, P. (1996). *Reform and resistance in schools and classrooms: An ethnographic view of the Coalition of Essential Schools.* New Haven, CT: Yale University Press.

Murphy, J. (1992). *Restructuring schools: Capturing and assessing the phenomena.* New York: Teachers College Press.

New American Schools Development Corporation. (1997). *Bringing success to scale: Sharing the vision of New American Schools.* Arlington, VA: Author.

New American Schools Development Corporation. (1999). *New American Schools: An update to the board of directors.* Presentation to the NAS Board of Directors, unpublished document. Arlington, VA: Author.

Newmann, F. M., & Associates (eds.) (1996). *Authentic achievement: Restructuring schools for intellectual quality.* San Francisco, CA: Jossey Bass.

Newmann, F., King, B., & Youngs, P. (2000). "Professional development that addresses school capacity." Paper presented at the annual meeting of the American Educational Research Association.

Newmann, F. M., Rutter, R. A., & Smith, M. S. (1989). "Organizational factors that affect school sense of efficacy, community, and expectations." *Sociology of education,* 51(4), pp. 221–238.

Newmann, F., & Wehlage, G. (1995). *Successful school restructuring.* Madison, WI: Center on Organization and Restructuring of Schools.

Nunnery, J. A. (1998). "Reform ideology and the locus of development problem in educational restructuring: Enduring lessons from studies of educational innovation." *Education and urban society,* 30(3), pp. 277–295.

Oakes, J. (1994). "More than misapplied technology: A normative and political response to Hallinan on tracking." *Sociology of education,* 67(2), pp. 84–88.

Oakes, J., Gamoran, A., & Page, R. N. (1992). "Curriculum differentiation: Opportunities, outcomes, and meanings." In P. W. Jackson. (ed.). *Handbook of research on curriculum,* New York: Macmillan, pp. 570–608.

Parsons, T. (1959). "The school class as a social system: Some of its functions in American society." *Harvard educational review,* 29, pp. 297–318.

Perrow, C. (1986). *Complex organizations: A critical essay, 3rd Edition.* New York: Random House.

Powell, A. G., Farrar, E., & Cohen, D. K. (1985). *The shopping mall high school: Winners and losers in the educational marketplace.* Boston, MA: Houghton Mifflen.

Purkey, S. C., & Smith, M. S. (1983). "Effective schools: A review." *The elementary school journal,* 83(4), pp. 427–452.

Ralph, J. (1990). "A research agenda on effective school for disadvantaged students." In *Readings on equal education,* vol. 10: *Critical issues for a new administration and Congress,* S. S. Goldberg (ed.). New York: AMS Press.

Rosenholtz, S. J. (1985). "Effective schools: Interpreting the evidence." *American journal of education,* 93, pp. 352–388.

Rosenholtz, S. J. (1989). *Teachers' workplace: The social organization of schools.* New York: Longman.

Ross, S., Troutman, A., Horgan, D., Maxwell, S., Laitinen, R., & Lowther, D. (1997). "The success of schools in implementing eight restructuring designs: A synthesis of first year evaluation outcomes." *School effectiveness and school improvement* 8(1), pp. 95–124.

Singer, J. D. (1998). "Using SAS PROC MIXED to fit multilevel models, hierarchical models, and individual growth models." *Journal of educational and behavioral statistics*, 24(4), pp. 323–355.

Sizer, T. R. (1984). *Horace's compromise: The dilemma of the American high school.* Boston, MA: Houghton Mifflin.

Slavin, R. E. (1987). "Ability grouping and student achievement in elementary schools: A best-evidence synthesis." *Review of educational research*, 57, pp. 293–336.

Slavin, R. E. (1990). "Achievement effects of ability grouping in secondary schools: A best-evidence synthesis." *Review of educational research*, 60, pp. 471–499.

Smith, L., Ross, S., McNelis, M., Squires, M., Wasson, R., Maxwell, S., Weddle, K., Nath, L., Grehan, A., & Buggey, T. (1998). "The Memphis restructuring initiative: Analyses of activities and outcomes that impact implementation success." *Education and urban society*, 30(3), pp. 296–325.

Smith, M. S., Scoll, B. W., & Link, J. (1996). "Research-based school reform: The Clinton administration's agenda." In E. A. Hanushek and D. W. Jorgenson (eds.). *Improving America's schools: The role of incentives.* Washington, DC: National Academy Press, pp. 9–27.

Stigler, J., & Hiebert, J. (1999). *The teaching gap.* New York: The Free Press.

Stringfield, S., & Datnow, A. (eds.) (1998). *Education and urban society*, 30(3).

Sykes, G. (1990). "Fostering teacher professionalism in schools." In R. F. Elmore (ed.). *Restructuring schools: The next generation of educational reform.* San Francisco, CA: Jossey-Bass.

Tyack, D., & Cuban, L. (1995). *Tinkering toward Utopia: A century of public school reform.* Cambridge, MA: Harvard University Press.

U.S. Department of Education (1993). *Improving America's Schools Act of 1993: The reauthorization of the Elementary and Secondary Education Act and other amendments.* Washington, DC: U.S. Department of Education.

Weatherly, R., & Lipsky, M. (1977). "Street level bureaucrats and institutional innovation: Implementing special education reform." *Harvard education review,* 47(2), pp. 171–197.

Wise, A. E. (1989). "Professional teaching: A new paradigm for the management of education." In T. J. Sergiovanni and J. H. Moore (eds.). *Schooling for tomorrow: Directing reforms to issues that count.* Boston, MA: Allyn and Bacon.

Wong, K. K., & Meyer, S. (1998). "An overview of Title I schoolwide programs: Federal legislative expectations." Philadelphia, PA: Mid-Atlantic Regional Education Laboratory at Temple University Center for Research in Human Development and Education.